The Promise of Long Term Recovery

John Frederick Zurn

Published by Everlasting Light, Yorkville, IL, 2023.

The Promise of Long Term Recovery
by John Frederick Zurn

Everlasting Light Publishing
    Yorkville, IL USA

https://www.portalstoinnerdimensions.com/[1]

Table of Contents

Dedication

I owe so much to so many people who have helped me along the way. I can't possibly repay them for their encouragement and support. This book is a small step in that direction.

I am deeply appreciative of the people at NAMI (National Alliance on Mental Illness) of DuPage for all their support. Their generosity and encouragement have given me the self-confidence to write and speak openly about my mental illness.

Introduction

As an individual with a diagnosis of bipolar disorder, I have spent most of my life coping with an illness that is very difficult to identify and extremely challenging to manage. For me, and millions of others, this illness continues to defy any comprehensive explanation. Recovery can be a life long process.

Even as medications continue to improve making life better for many, the illness itself still has no known cure. This dilemma has left many of us coping with bipolar disorder feeling healthy enough to function, but still sick enough to face recurring symptoms. Over the years, we have undergone any number of treatments in hospitals and other mental health settings, seeking relief and the promise of long term recovery. With the help of mental health professionals, family, and our own perseverance, many of us have diligently worked for a chance to live a life of purpose with a renewed sense of inner strength and courage.

As my own long term recovery endures, I have the opportunity to share my ideas and experiences with others. In my books, *The Bipolar Challenge* and *Memoirs of a Bipolar Soul*, I have written about my life in some detail and given some suggestions about symptom management. Since then, I have also given many presentations as a speaker for the DuPage County affiliate of the National Alliance on Mental Illness (NAMI). During these presentations, I continue to share my story and exchange ideas with others. These presentations have been in locations like hospitals, middle schools, high schools, colleges, universities, a medical school, nursing schools, support groups, senior centers, and police trainings.

During these presentations certain topics repeatedly surface that deeply interest individuals with bipolar disorder, their families, and mental health professionals. These discussions have challenged my own perceptions and deepened my understanding of the illness and its effect on everyone encountering it. After giving a number of these talks, I realized these recurring themes could be expanded upon far beyond the limits of my other books.

In this book, *The Promise of Long Term Recovery*, I share some of my ideas that reflect a more in depth look at some of the challenges many of us face. These challenges include some pressing and persistent problems associated with long term recovery and solutions that promote inner stability and growth.

I characterize some of the differences in viewpoints among mental health professionals, families, and individuals in regard to the treatment of bipolar disorder. These sources of disagreement include the way in which psychological concepts like "behavior modification" and "religiosity" define mental illness in restrictive ways.

The purpose is to examine the symptoms of bipolar disorder with a fresh perspective. Resisting the temptation to categorize thoughts, feelings, and actions as merely "psychotic" or "delusional", more subtle explanations for symptoms emerge. While underscoring the essential need for medications, counseling, and coping skills, bipolar disorder also presents an opportunity for creative expression and spiritual evolution.

In this effort to expand on some traditional beliefs about bipolar disorder, delusional states are described as having underlying significance for individuals, even though these states of mind are largely dismissed by some mental health professionals.

These symptoms do, in fact, provide some sense of purpose for those of us with a mental illness. I believe these symptoms may continue to manifest until these thoughts are addressed - medically and psychologically, as well as creatively and spiritually.

This book is not a debate about whether bipolar disorder is a major illness or not. Nor does it suggest that will power and creativity alone can take the place of medication and counseling. Anyone with a real understanding of, or experience with, this illness would surely reject such misguided assumptions. Rather, it expands upon the interpretation of symptoms to include them as subtle clues identifying a deeper yearning that cannot be developed without a balanced lifestyle.

<u>The book is in three parts:</u>

Part 1: A brief autobiography provides some relevant background and context

Part 2: (Chapters 2 through 11)

Ideas and principles many people seem interested in discussing. They include these topics: medication, coping skills, psychology, creativity, and spirituality. This part offers many unique and potentially useful ideas and attitudes that can help provide direction and promote self-discovery.

There is a bit of repetition for important concepts like medication, counseling and employment. Since some may choose to "skip around" as they read, some essential points are restated along the way.

THE PROMISE OF LONG TERM RECOVERY

Part 3: A sci-fi fantasy novella - *Mystery of the Thought Healer*.

It expands upon some of the concepts explored in the book. Abstract ideas about psychology, creativity, and spirituality are "brought to life" so to speak, by the interaction of plots, characters, and themes reflecting these subtle principles.

The ideas in this book are based on my own interactions, beliefs, and experiences. I hope they will be useful to others like me, or at the very least, provide some explanations for those who so earnestly wish to understand and help us.

A note about vocabulary. In the mental health world a patient is sometimes referred to as a "consumer". I use that terminology in many places.

1. Brief Autobiography

My story begins when I was fourteen years old growing up in upstate New York. At that time, the legal drinking age was eighteen. Most of the seniors in high school were eighteen. They frequently sponsored "keg parties" for a fee of a dollar or two, as well as purchasing alcohol for others. There was an active market in making and selling fake id for underage students. Throughout high school we drank every weekend during the school year and all summer.

I was a pretty good student, played the trumpet, and ran cross-country and track. At graduation, I was awarded a partial scholarship to St. John Fisher College in Rochester, New York.

But in the summer of my freshman year, I had a life changing experience. While I was jogging around the lake at my uncle's resort, I became violently ill with severe cramps. By the time I arrived at the hospital the next day, I had to have an emergency appendectomy. Back in 1974, if my appendix would have burst, I surely would have died. So, for the first time, I realized that death was both real and inescapable. Over time, I became obsessed with death and lost interest in almost everything as depression overwhelmed me.

Eventually, when the depression finally lifted, I experienced, what could be described as three consecutive "manic" episodes. During these "psychotic breaks", I deliberately raced my thoughts as fast as possible seeking answers to my questions about death. During all three episodes, I was hospitalized for months at a time. Since my symptoms were manic, I was consistently misdiagnosed as a consumer (patient) with schizophrenia.

Two years later, I made a very serious suicide attempt; I was a patient in intensive care for about a week. Ironically, that desperate act provided the vital information to correctly reach my diagnosis of bipolar disorder. (Based on my experience some of my younger relatives have also been diagnosed with bipolar disorder as well without the usual trial and error process.)

Unfortunately, once I had the correct diagnosis, I wasn't willing to take the medications. I believed that I was strong enough and had enough faith to do without them. I continued relying on alcohol for problem solving, stress management, and self-confidence.

Not surprisingly, several years later, I began to get into trouble. Once, in a delusional state, I drove through Schaumburg, Illinois, ignoring stop lights and street signs, while traveling at a high rate of speed. When the police officers cornered me in the Woodfield Shopping Mall parking lot, I was taken to Elgin Mental Health Center. I was a resident there three different times for months at a time. While living there, I took whatever medications the psychiatrist prescribed for me. Every time I was discharged, I gradually stopped taking all of them.

Then, I got into very serious trouble. I hired a cab from Elgin to Champaign for two-hundred and fifty dollars, so I could visit my brother at college. Since my brother was more interested in studying than partying, we parted company, and I ran out of money. Eventually, a university mental health counselor gave me a bus ticket to Chicago. When I arrived, I began wandering the downtown streets. At about 2 a.m., I began directing and blocking traffic because I believed I was the fifth Beatle*, and that one of the group members was coming to pick me up. *[The Beatles were a world-famous rock group from the mid-sixties to the early seventies.]*

People from a nearby bar threw bottles at me; a man tackled me. The police came. I was taken to the psych division of Cook County Jail called Cermak, a vicious, brutal place. After four or five days, two officers pushed me out the front door. I had no belt or shoes and was told to "behave myself".

I wandered around the Chicago area for a while. I was again incarcerated, this time in another section of Cook County Jail. I was picked up because I missed the court date for the Woodfield incident.

This jail was a violent world of savagery and despair. I didn't think I would survive it.

Acceptance, for me, has been a process over time. I finally realized that taking medication was a safety issue. I would need to take medications if I were to have any chance of leading a normal life. I began to understand that bipolar disorder is not caused by any weakness or character flaw. It's a biological disorder of the brain. For me, that means taking medication.

Medications have allowed me to remain independent. Without them, I eventually get sick and others are required to make all my important life decisions. Mental health professionals and relatives would be required to decide: where I would live, what medications I would take, where I might work, and even how I might structure my day. Medications have actually given me *more* independence not less.

However, medications aren't "magic beans" either. Family, friends, and mental health professionals all want closure. They want medications to solve every problem. Yet, even while taking medication as prescribed, it sometimes requires a Herculean effort to manage symptoms, deal with side effects, and overcome discrimination.

Since the medicine is considered a panacea, self-effort is marginalized, even though it is as at least as important as the medications themselves. For me, this led to humiliation, alienation, and non-cooperation.

Another psychological issue I had to grapple with after I finally accepted medications, was the complete change of attitude that was required. When I began taking medications faithfully, I had to acknowledge that I was a consumer with bipolar disorder. This was very difficult to integrate into my sense of self-esteem, creativity, and spirituality.

Over time, I have come to accept and appreciate the value of counseling. I didn't go to counseling because I was a weak person or because my wife and I didn't get along. I went to counseling because bipolar disorder is a very difficult obstacle to handle. First, I needed to learn about the illness. Next, I had to understand how it affected me. Finally, I had to learn how it affected my relationships.

There are many challenges consumers face, requiring developing of complex strategies to resolve. These include: job discrimination, insurance problems, sleep difficulties, unemployment, medication issues, and even the day to day art of living. Overall, my wife Donna and I have greatly benefited from counselors who were able to help us overcome these formidable obstacles.

One of the most difficult things for me has been changing my lifestyle. I had to phase out drinking alcohol completely. I needed to develop specific routines in the areas of sleep, meditation, and exercise. Because of my mental challenges, I also had to accept some limitations in the areas of employment, recreation, and relationships.

In addition to medication, counseling, and lifestyle changes, I developed some helpful, positive attitudes.

First, I learned to forgive and forget. Over the years, because of many negative experiences, I had constant thoughts of anger, resentment, and the desire for justice. However, all these painful thoughts and feelings of injustice were slowly poisoning my life. So, after counseling, I decided to give them up like unwanted baggage.

Next, I learned to forgive myself and learn from my mistakes. Instead of focusing on missed opportunities, I now try to live in the present and do my best.

Third, I learned to be grateful. When I was younger I thought I was completely on my own. Now I realize a lot of people helped me along the way, and they're still helping me now. This has given me a new perspective.

Finally, I had to learn humility. Taking medication has been a very humbling experience for me. Many people see medicine as a sign of weakness and as a lack of courage. I know these attitudes are true because I once had them as well.

Now, when I give presentations, and in my writing, I stress the importance of medications. One image I like is a sandcastle. I can build and reinforce a castle with strategies like jogging, meditation, and creative writing. However, when a wave of mental illness strikes without medication, the castle washes away.

Individuals with mental illness have many societal hurdles as well. In our culture, support and opposition coexist, making advocacy really important. Attitudes about mental illness still come primarily from the media - an important source of our information, education, and entertainment. It continues to create stereotypes and sustain prejudicial attitudes. Mental illness is one of the last remaining subjects television can openly ridicule without fear of consequences, although that has started to change in recent years.

So, while we wait for more effective medications, more comprehensive therapies, and a more compassionate society, we are forced into higher stress, lower paying jobs, no one else wants. While we walk around with an elephant strapped to our backs, society is indifferent or worse. Even today, young people are stranded and forgotten in nursing homes, jails, and living on the street; they are neither seen nor heard, often hiding in plain sight.

Our society needs to understand mental illnesses are physical disorders of the brain. When that fact is understood, there will be more research, funding, and advocacy. Compassion and empathy are important, but there is no substitute for knowledge.

Mental illness is very treatable. The National Alliance on Mental Illness (NAMI) offers support, education, and advocacy. Consumers and their families need not struggle alone.

THE PROMISE OF LONG TERM RECOVERY

Bipolar disorder no longer rules my relationships and dominates my life. Instead, it has made me a more creative and compassionate person. By accepting my illness, I have become more disciplined and productive because I better understand and manage my thoughts and feelings. With the help of my wife, Donna, I now cherish the life I once considered worthless.

Over the years, I've taught elementary school, middle school, and high school. In addition, I've taught refugees and students with autism. I was employed as a psychosocial rehabilitation counselor for a number of years, assisting adults dually diagnosed with two mental challenges. When I couldn't find a teaching job, I worked as a stock room manager, house cleaner, and factory worker.

I have written and published books on mental health as well as several novels, collections of poetry and short stories.

2. Making Decisions about Medications

Acceptance and Adjustment

One of the most significant issues facing individuals with bipolar disorder involves the choices we make about medications. Such major issues as acceptance, effectiveness, and side effects are almost always at the center of these concerns, and usually create the greatest challenges. Often, there are vast differences in the attitudes of the families and their mentally ill relatives concerning the need for medications, especially when these medications are prescribed over an extended period of time.

One of the main reasons for this long, sometimes intense, debate, is the genuine anxiety and doubt individuals with bipolar disorder experience about taking medications. These feelings of apprehension can be minimized or even ignored by mental health professionals and families. Medication decisions are often made in emergency situations. They are presented in a persuasive manner seeking to solve the immediate crisis. The problem, however, is the individual who is ill sometimes has no real power in the decision making process even after the initial emergency has passed. This whole sequence of events does little to allay the individuals fears and legitimate concerns as they confront the implications of medication and the burden of a diagnosis that may last a lifetime.

Consequently, I believe that discussing these medication issues from the individual's view point may help highlight their valid objections. Listening to the individual's concerns and sincerely addressing them, makes it far more likely the medications will be accepted as an important part of treatment and long term recovery. Equally important, these ideas may also help foster a greater understanding and genuine empathy in others involved in the whole recovery process. This overall attitude change by all concerned could, in turn, help sustain a more supportive environment with genuine understanding.

One of the most common concerns and contentious issues is the individual's willingness to take medication on a regular basis. There are many reasons specific to individuals. There are also important explanations common to many which aren't always easily discernable. For example, one of the most deeply felt explanations for avoiding medication, is our culture's insistence on viewing individuals with bipolar disorder in moral and judgmental terms - interpreting symptoms as character flaws, personal weaknesses, or as evidence of a lack of faith. When individuals acknowledge their disorder and take medication, they must endure society's stigma and discrimination. Tragically, these widely held attitudes create a deep and lasting scar that individuals with bipolar disorder may carry with them for years. The illness itself is difficult enough to manage without the added stress of societal ignorance.

In the minds of many of us who were initially uncooperative regarding medication, the thinking usually went something like this:

> *If I don't accept the diagnosis or the medications, then I don't have the disease. This, in turn, allows me to escape stigma, discrimination, and humiliation.*

Of course, this logic is horribly flawed and can be potentially life threatening; but it is surely understandable. The point is that accepting the illness necessitates accepting all the difficulties that go with it.

Ironically, for many years, I held these same ignorant beliefs about mental illness. Because of my own pride and sense of determination, I believed will power and faith could take the place of medication. For me, finally acknowledging I was an individual with a bipolar disorder, required accepting the primary importance of medications. In doing so, I radically altered my belief system. My self-esteem, identity, and even my spirituality were deeply affected. My feelings of self-worth and independence were constantly threatened by uncertainties about my mental health. I felt I was constantly cast in the role of patient; it began to smother my identity.

Even more distressing were my thoughts about creativity and spirituality. With each hospitalization, my mind became so tangled up that I seriously doubted my imagination would ever return. Still more disconcerting was the profound effect my illness had on my religious beliefs. Thoughts, feelings and spiritual experiences I once considered authentic were now diagnosed as psychotic. My self-esteem plummeted. At that time, this fear led me to believe that medications blocked or even disconnected my links to creativity and spirituality, giving me a legitimate reason for discontinuing medications.

It has been known for years that any attitude change, like as accepting a mental illness, may take a long time. Even accepting changes in beliefs like voting for a specific political candidate or deciding on a career change, take time to be accepted and internalized. So it seems unrealistic to expect individuals with bipolar disorder to immediately accept their new situation, although it would be exceedingly courageous and helpful if they did.

Mental health professionals and families seek *immediate* acceptance and cooperation from those of us with bipolar disorder for a number of valid reasons. The issue of safety cannot be overstated. The illness is so difficult to manage that without medications, dangerous situations can evolve that are career damaging and life threatening.

Social networks can be strained to the breaking point causing isolation, alienation, and embarrassment.

Financial resources can be depleted very quickly when there is no available insurance, or when benefits run out. Since it takes time and money to correctly diagnose and successfully treat bipolar disorder, individuals and their families often go into debt for years, spending tens of thousands of dollars. This only adds to the tremendous stress everyone experiences during this difficult period of acceptance and adjustment.

Psychiatrists seek long term cooperation from individuals when it comes to medications. Usually, after a long and agonizing trial and error period, the appropriate medications are finally identified. When individuals stop taking their medication (as I often did, even after being correctly diagnosed) the psychiatrist has to de-escalate the crisis and carefully manage medications again. Families caught up in this repeating cycle are understandably deeply concerned about relapse.

This whole issue about acceptance of medication goes far beyond our personal responsibility. In fact, many of the problems individuals with bipolar disorder face are mostly unknown to others. For example, part of long term recovery, social integration, and economic survival require us to lead a kind of double life. We rarely disclose our mental challenges to anyone, especially employers or perspective employers.

I have never found employment, or even heard of anyone, who found a job by disclosing information about their diagnosis. There were times when I was denied a job after interviewers stumbled upon my mental health background, even after I had successfully passed preliminary background checks. On job applications themselves, I believe, any box that pertains to mental illness will immediately disqualify a candidate from employment because the infamous "affirmative action" box actually serves as a red flag. Unfortunately, acceptance is not yet a two way street.

For individuals with bipolar disorder, many career opportunities are really not available. Often, we must take jobs no one else wants. Jobs which typically pay less, and have greater levels of stress. These positions, usually needing to be filled, often have less extensive reference checks. It has been my experience, that individuals with bipolar disorder have the ability to be excellent workers but are often not given the chance to prove themselves. For me, once I engaged with Chipmunka Publishing and NAMI (The National Alliance on Mental Illness-DuPage), I finally had genuine opportunities to share my thoughts and ideas with others. It gave me the courage to share my "secret" outside of therapy.

Individuals with bipolar disorder who do accept their illness and persevere enough to find some kind of employment, are very reluctant to discuss their illness and medications at work. This becomes self-defeating, if they begin to manifest symptoms. When this happens, many of us either quit before we have a major episode, or struggle alone, hoping our medications and coping skills improve our situation. If the situation continues to deteriorate, we may endure the "walk of shame" as we are escorted from the building while our former coworkers stop and stare.

Another hidden, deeply rooted obstacle individuals with bipolar manic depression must face: if they accept their illness, there is the societal notion that courage and faith are always appropriate solutions in *every* circumstance. These values are often rigorously applied to individuals with mental illness, but not so much for people with other diseases and medical conditions. If individuals with bipolar disorder become ill, we are accused of lacking courage and faith. If various medicines and therapies are ineffective, we are told to "have more patience and more faith". If we still don't get well, it was because we didn't have "enough" courage and faith. Soon, these subtle accusations become more direct and generalized into overall behavioral themes like lack of motivation (laziness), self-involvement (selfishness), and noncompliance (stubbornness).

Even while we attempt to follow through with various medications, society itself is clearly sending us a mixed message: "If you were strong enough and had enough faith and determination, you wouldn't need the medications; but since you're not, you have to take them."

These prevailing attitudes – which I encountered repeatedly – clearly demonstrate that bipolar disorder is still not understood to be a physical disorder of the brain. Even those who assert that they do recognize it as a physical illness, still tend to fall back on easy explanations and all too familiar stereotypes. For example, when the illness doesn't respond to treatment, the individual is often blamed for lack of perseverance and for seeking attention.

My own experience has been that mental illness is far more difficult to manage than other health problems. For example, when I fractured my ankle and later broke a rib, I was very surprised to realize that my bipolar disorder symptoms were much more painful and difficult to diagnose and treat. My feelings of isolation and anxiety were intense and unintelligible to others. It was apparent no one really understood my thoughts and feelings.

Finding the right combination of medications was exceedingly difficult. At times, being mentally ill was like speaking a foreign language that was totally unintelligible to others, only adding to my frustration and mistrust. On the other hand, the ankle and rib fractures, were x-rayed, diagnosed, and treated in a very short period of time. The whole process was extremely objective and easily managed. I was treated with dignity, respect, and understanding.

This difference in diagnostic procedures is one of the important reasons for individual and societal discrimination. For most physical illnesses there are reliable procedures like blood tests, x-rays, and MRI exams. These diagnostic tools are scientific in approach and objectively verifiable. By contrast, the diagnosis for bipolar disorder is highly subjective and based on the presence of a collection of symptoms and, more recently, family histories. This necessitates collecting, interpreting, and diagnosing the symptoms based on sometimes unreliable observers and incomplete family records. Because this process is in some ways "unscientific," members of society create their own explanations, which are rarely supportive and sometimes cruel. Strangely enough, even though there is a vast amount of evidence to demonstrate that bipolar disorder does run in families, it is still only suggested as a possibility and not a scientific fact.

This constant uncertainty about diagnosis, medication, and cooperation makes long term recovery challenging. Since bipolar disorder often strikes suddenly and forcefully, it becomes a harrowing experience for all concerned. While psychiatrists painstakingly seek answers, the family is terrified and disbelieving; the individual with the illness is very sick and often traumatized. As emergency strategies are enacted, medications are prescribed in order to at least stabilize the desperately ill patient. Even when individuals begin to recover and take their illness seriously by trusting the process, there are always challenges in fine-tuning the medications. This trial and error process can be frustrating and can be more difficult than the diagnostic process itself.

It can actually take *years* to accurately identify and successfully treat bipolar disorder. Psychiatrists often encounter one pole of the illness - the manic phase or depressed phase - and so don't observe the entire cycle. Understandably, they may misdiagnose individuals with either schizophrenia or major depression. In my case, it took a nearly fatal suicide attempt to change my diagnosis away from schizophrenia. Tragically, by the time the correct diagnosis is finally made, frustration and humiliation of both the frediduals and their families can be devastating. Some may finally give up on treatment entirely.

When the correct diagnosis is finally discovered, the process of finding the appropriate medications becomes an ongoing ordeal. As brain chemistry changes and the environment shifts, medication changes may be necessary.

As this painful process unfolds, it becomes difficult to resist the temptation to assign blame due to the lack of success with medications and symptom management. This sometimes occurs in so-called talk therapies. These individual and group therapies are exceedingly useful in understanding relationships, discovering thought patterns, and acquiring coping skills; however, they may be limiting and deceptive by overlooking the primary importance of medications and individual differences.

It is unfair to require individuals and their families to assume blame for their lack of progress in their relationships, when the real culprit is the underlying *biological* brain disorder. Symptoms often appear very early in life. The lack of understanding among family members can be interpreted, at least partially, in terms of the individual's symptoms and interactions within the family, rather than "blaming" the parents for an individual's difficult childhood. In the end, when it is discovered that no one is to blame, the revelation can be enormously helpful.

This entire process requires more than a submissive willingness on the part of the individual to take medication. The person must be actively engaged in finding and adjusting medications over a lifetime. A forced acceptance that is based partly on coercion may be a first step, but in the long term recovery process, a strong determination to follow through on medications is vital. It is truly humbling to accept the notion that we as individuals with bipolar disorder cannot totally control our own minds because of a biological brain disorder. However, it is often an essential step in the recovery process.

This issue of constantly evaluating medications was made clear to me, yet again, a number of years ago. One of the medications I'd been prescribed for a very long period of time was identified as a source of concern. It was determined that I might need to stop taking off that specific medication. Secretly, I was eager to pursue this course of action, because I believed I might be able to discontinue its use and perhaps discontinue other medications as well.

For about two weeks I felt fine; but then I began to relapse. Even while employing thirty years of coping strategies, I still became ill and was nearly hospitalized. As the situation deteriorated, I fell back into negative thought patterns and attempted to blame various external situations, and even loved ones, as the causes for my difficult thoughts and feelings. Fortunately, the problem was resolved, and I was able to resume taking the medication. This experience was humbling and disappointing. It reminded me how vulnerable I am without medications and a support system.

Certainly, when most individuals with bipolar disorder struggle with medications, regardless of the circumstances, their problems can be subtle and easily misinterpreted. Even when individuals patiently endure the trial and error phase of treatment, they often struggle alone. Frequently, mental health professionals and friends have a limited insight into the individual's suffering because they have no frame of reference. The belief, for example, that mania is euphoric doesn't take into account other symptoms of mania, like extreme paranoia, that can result in totally misreading situations. It is stated that mania includes racing thoughts and the reduced need for sleep. In actuality, the racing thoughts are uncontrollable; they create overwhelming fear and intense anxiety. As to sleep, it is more accurate to describe mania as *the <u>inability to sleep</u>*. This can create a horrible state of mind that makes everything else worse. These symptoms can lead individuals to commit suicide if they cannot endure these intensely manic states. Professionals can't identify with the experience itself; so their attempts to understand, while important, are sometimes limited.

Even some of the more apparent obstacles that individuals struggle with can be largely forgotten or glossed over by those around them. In addition to taking medications as prescribed, individuals with bipolar disorder still must manage symptoms, contend with side effects, and handle the additional stress that comes with the diagnosis.

The most important misconception is the perception that the medications are "magic potions" that solve every problem. This ignores the tremendous patience, courage, and self-effort involved with coping with the illness as a whole. It is a frustrating experience when the medications receive *all* the credit for progress and the individual's hard work is marginalized or ignored. It is a degrading and humiliating experience to work so hard at staying well with so little genuine understanding. I strongly suspect many individuals are far less willing to stay on medications when their self-effort is ignored.

Medications can make everything else possible; but guarantee nothing. *They just give us the chance to lead a productive life.*

Together with acceptance, effectiveness is a primary concern for everyone. Sometimes medications don't work well for a person, or they don't work over an extended period of time. Tragically, for some individuals, no medications seem to be much help, despite the best efforts of all concerned.

I remember a situation a number of years ago, that developed where I was employed. There were a number of residents in an institution, who were very positively affected by a new medication that literally transformed their lives for a long period of time. Sadly, after a number of years, the same medication proved ineffective for some.

Another prevailing tragic condition, is the number of young people occupying entire floors in nursing homes. They have almost no independence. I suspect there are often no medications that help them. This ineffectiveness of the medications is verifiable only by observing residents who are required to take medications and still aren't doing well. Sadly, society labels these individuals as "chronic". They are viewed as responsible for their fate because "they won't take their medication". While this may be true for some, it mostly serves to appease our social conscience.

It seems clear that solutions for medication effectiveness should focus more on research, innovation, and compassion rather than on fault finding and stereotypical explanations. There is no substitute for knowledge. For individuals with mental illness, it has been a very long wait.

For most of us with bipolar disorder, medication effectiveness can be described as helpful as part of an overall solution. Since each individual's experience is unique, our mental health depends on a variety of factors. For most of us, the effectiveness of our medications can be lightheartedly compared to a jalopy that we're driving down the street. We chug along, backfire, and occasionally stall, but we still keep driving forward. Sometimes the stresses on the road with its cracks and potholes can wear us down. But, without the medications, we would most certainly be abandoned on the side of the road.

Side Effects - Physical

Together with acceptance and effectiveness, side effects are a major source of conflict and anxiety for individuals with bipolar disorder. This illness often strikes in the late teens and early twenties. The medications prescribed for these young adults invariably come with side effects that directly impact some of the most vulnerable aspects of their lives. These side effects can be so socially unacceptable that the medications are sometimes dropped altogether. For example, it is not at all uncommon for an individual on medications to gain thirty or forty pounds in just a few months. This gained weight can be very difficult to take off and keep off for any length of time. For a young person, this is really difficult to tolerate especially when the weight is often lost again when the medications are discontinued.

Other significant medication side effects affecting some include: dry mouth, restlessness, stiffness, drowsiness, and lethargy. Less common, but more troubling side effects may occur in the trial and error stage of treatment. The list is virtually endless. They are real and pose a significant challenge for individuals managing symptoms, particularly when they involve long term side effects that are to some degree unknown.

Side Effects - Relationships

Beyond the physical side effects, there are social side effects involving activities like dating, drinking alcohol, and education. The desire to sustain a long term relationship, for example, is often difficult for individuals with mental illness because at some point, they will have to reveal their "secret". Then the illness can become an integral part of the couple's relationship, if the relationship survives at all. It is true mental illness can bring couples together; it can also create a strain, emotionally and financially. Fortunately, my wife Donna's unconditional love, support, and her ability to navigate through the mental health system has brought us closer together despite the circumstances.

The problems with relationships, go beyond dating and marriage. With mental illness, all social relationships are usually affected in some way. Virtually every time I became ill, I lost friends and coworkers because of my symptoms. This caused a great deal of stress and humiliation for me especially when my "secret" life became apparent for all to witness. In time, as I began to think about my need for recognition, I finally developed a helpful strategy for dealing with the social effects of my illness. If people don't accept or respect me, my silent response is "the heck with them". The truth is that once people get to know me, my mental challenges aren't a problem at all - unless I become ill again.

Alcohol

One of the most insidious social obstacles is alcohol. It thrives almost everywhere in our culture; for someone with bipolar disorder it can be a significant obstacle to overcome. Our society uses alcohol to celebrate virtually everything: sporting events, holidays, birthdays, anniversaries, promotions, friendships, midterms, finals, victories, defeats, and even days of the week. Alcohol is almost unavoidable in our daily lives, and it can be very difficult to turn down in every social setting. Since it is a major part of our social dynamic, being an individual with bipolar disorder becomes more difficult by society's relentless consumption of liquor. Sadly, Donna and I don't attend a lot of social gatherings at all anymore. For me, it was no fun watching everyone else get intoxicated while I drank club soda.

Our society uses alcohol to manage stress and for recreation. If individuals with a mental illness take medication, how can they be seen as weak and lacking courage when many people use alcohol to enhance self-esteem, relieve stress, and manage anxiety? The fact is that many members of society cannot do without alcohol, not for just a day, or a month, much less for good. Many individuals with bipolar disorder who take medications don't "get high", ever. How <u>do</u> we define weakness?

Some individuals with an undiagnosed mental illness use alcohol and drugs to manage their symptoms. It is logical that if mental illnesses were more acceptable to society, those struggling individuals would be more likely to seek treatment. This revelation could help them understand many of the underlying, contributing factors for their alcohol and substance abuse issues.

Education

For those of us with a mental illness, the process of education can be a very difficult challenge with daunting obstacles and uncertainties most other students don't encounter. Low self-esteem and managing symptoms like depression frequently add to the already constant stresses of paying for school and earning a certificate, diploma or degree.

Losing time because of incomplete and dropped classes, due to hospitalizations and long absences, can sometimes feel like having the future stolen. As this sense of falling behind is felt more intensely, the strategy of leading a "double life" brings doubt and alienation. The almost unbearable loneliness and isolation can cause many of us to forget about school entirely.

I was very fortunate in terms of support at Western Illinois University. Although I had to drop out at times, there were counselors and faculty members who were very caring. The university had a good health care system. I was eventually able to earn my degree by returning periodically. Nevertheless, it is also true that many students have much more difficulty getting help during their college years than I did.

Time of Life Impacts

One of the core issues for individuals with bipolar disorder is the timing of the onset of the disease. Since it usually manifests during the late teens and early twenties – during the height of social involvement – it clashes with the need for independence and self-sufficiency. Maturing youths have just left home and have gone to college, joined the military, or entered the work force. After being supervised for their entire lives, these individuals are now finally on their own, creating their own lives, and doing the things they choose to do. This includes independently establishing their own relationships, pursuing their own goals, and exploring their own beliefs.

Suddenly, like lightning, the illness strikes... In many cases, almost immediately, individuals with bipolar disorder lose control of their destiny. They may drop out of school, the military, lose their jobs and living places. They often are home, again under constant supervision. Now, everyone wants to give them advice including family members, mental health professionals, and friends. Just when their feelings of independence and self-confidence have brought hope and freedom, their world collapses around them. Unexpectedly these individuals are required to accept a major mental illness as an integral part of their daily lives. Every plan is then on hold or abandoned; slowly, more "realistic" goals replace them. No longer in control of their own future, there is more supervision and regulation than ever before.

The awful irony of these tragic situations is that individuals with bipolar disorder usually <u>do</u> need help to successfully manage their illness. So, even while they are desperately seeking independence, they probably cannot realize this goal without accepting help and counseling. Even still, it is difficult to feel empowered when medications and counseling are replacing independent initiative and self-discovery.

Quality of Life

In addition to the problems of acceptance, effectiveness, and medical\ social side effects; medications impact an individual's quality of life. If taking medication doesn't offer substantive relief and help sustain a genuine sense of purpose, they are of little value. The medications may make individuals more cooperative, but they certainly don't always encourage inner growth and development, particularly when stigma and discrimination are factored in.

These needs for hope and purpose are crucial for everyone, of course, but probably more so for individuals with mental illness, who have repeatedly experienced disappointment and despair. Taking medication may be the vital first step required for individuals seeking to realize their hopes and dreams, but it probably isn't enough. If, thereafter, the individual is still unsuccessful in finding meaningful work and supportive relationships, then medication and self-effort may seem pointless. Sometimes individuals with bipolar disorder give up altogether until the environment becomes more promising and their courage returns.

Courage and a sense of purpose are not always enough. Loneliness and boredom are very destructive, yet ignored as problems. It is difficult to describe without a frame of reference; mental illness can be very isolating and provide little substantive hope. Rejection by employers, friends, and others lead to despair at times. Even with medication, it is tragic so many intelligent, hard working individuals are still unsuccessful because they have been forgotten and left behind.

There are still more complex and emotionally charged issues concerning the medications themselves when they are considered as part of a long term solution. Because many individuals with bipolar disorder are creatively gifted; they are concerned about the way medications may inhibit or block their creative intelligence. I will address this in a later chapter; for now, I will briefly outline the problem.

There does seem to be a significant correlation between bipolar disorder and creativity, as any internet search of famous people with bipolar disorder will reveal. [See Chapter: *Famous People with Bipolar Disorder*]

There is a genuine fear among individuals considering a long term commitment to medication that their emotions will be muted and their creative energy thwarted. Since self-expression and seeking truth are often very high priorities for artists and for many other people, medications represent a possible threat to creative endeavors. As medications attempt to stabilize moods and restore thought processes, many individuals worry about losing their creativity entirely.

An important and related challenge associated with medications and bipolar disorder, is the belief that medications stifle spiritual thought and inhibit spiritual experience. I will address this in a later chapter. It is important to mention here

since it represents another major concern about medications that individuals sometimes experience. A root cause of this concern, I think, is the belief that God and faith can ultimately cure bipolar disorder without the need for medications. This belief strongly implies that if individuals don't get well their faith isn't strong enough. Even worse, if they become very ill, delusions are seen as real manifestations of some "evil spirit" at work. I experienced this belief and its expressions first-hand.

The reliance solely on faith instead of medications has validity for some, but it is also partially based on the misconception that mental illnesses are fundamentally different from other physical illnesses. There are few people who would even suggest that someone with a fractured arm or a case of pneumonia ignore medical treatment. However, those of us suffering with mental illnesses are treated as if our disease is curable without trusting in scientific advances. The fact that this topic is still actively debated, demonstrates that discrimination persists in the attitudes and behavior of many when discussing mental illness and medication.

Why Medications?

So, given all these problems with medications, why would individuals with bipolar disorder be willing to take medications at all? Even more importantly, why would they agree to take these medications over an extended period of time? At first glance, the evidence seems overwhelming that the risks are too great, and that the benefits are hardly worth the effort.

There are many, many excellent reasons for including medications as an integral part of an overall long term recovery strategy.

To begin with, it is absolutely essential to realize that bipolar disorder is a *physical disorder* of the brain, and the illness is not our fault. While we must inevitably take responsibility for managing it, it isn't something we caused or deserve. Despite society's mistaken notions and attitudes, it is a genetic disease and not the result of any character flaw or weakness. While self-effort is crucial, the illness is no different than any other physical illness when it comes to using medications..

I have never heard of a doctor who advised against taking medication for serious infections, or counseled a patient to use determination alone to fight cancer.

The truth is that bipolar disorder is a physical brain disorder with symptoms that manifest through thoughts and feelings. In other words, the cause is physical and the symptoms are psychological.

This area of societal ignorance is a major obstacle to overcome. Many of us with bipolar disorder have had to ignore society and well intentioned friends who often give bad advice. When we follow their advice and stop taking medications and symptoms re-emerge, this same society treats us like "throw away people" These well intentioned friends are never around when we get into dangerous situations because we were persuaded that we didn't need our medications.

I take medications and have done so for over thirty years because they provide a vital safety net. This decision has greatly improved my quality of life. By following through with them, I am very independent and make all my own life decisions. Before, when I would eventually become ill, my relatives and mental health professionals would need to make all my decisions; I wasn't independent at all. All the major decisions were made by others: where I would live, what job I might apply for, and even what medications I would take. These restrictions often led to a lack of genuine opportunity and a feeling of powerlessness.

Even with all my personal strategies and coping skills to help, medications are still vital for me. The illness isn't my fault, but its management is my responsibility. When I give presentations to various groups, I sometimes explain my situation using a sand castle on the beach as a metaphor. I can create this castle with various techniques: writing, meditation, jogging, nutrition, relaxation tapes, and inspirational reading. These coping skills are important and very valuable. However, without medication, whenever a powerful surge of mental illness crashes on to the shore, it washes my coping skill castle away almost effortlessly.

In the end, when I was ill, it was beyond my control, and the illness didn't announce its arrival until it was too late. When I was ill, I was almost never aware of it until I was finally tricked or man-handled into some hospital or institution.

The Truth is Simple and Clear to Me Now...

By accepting my illness, taking medications, and learning various coping skills, I have been able to radically change my life. This long term recovery has freed my wife and family from the frightening recurring circumstances whenever I became ill. Now, I'm able to participate fully in life with the chance to learn and grow beyond the threat of losing control.

This long term recovery has included the ability to remain self-confident while keeping my self-esteem intact. One of the biggest problems I faced with becoming ill was the need to continually "start from scratch" when it came to careers, relationships, and housing. Every time I lost a job, I had to be creative with my resume. A year and a half in an institution or halfway house don't provide marketable job references. Most relationships were strained or lost. Now, the medications and lasting relationships have allowed me to live a stable, productive, and creative life. It is very difficult at times, but far more fulfilling than it was.

A Few More Words on Challenges

The challenges with medications go beyond the will to follow through with them. There are many obstacles that appear that need to be overcome. This requires perseverance. By being engaged in the process, the optimal medication combinations can usually be found.

Another problem concerns the way medications affect an individual's life in general. If they work poorly or are seriously affecting an individual's quality of life, different combinations are usually available. However, if the medications are working well, and there is just one bothersome side effect, there may be ways to minimize its impact. If weight gain is the problem, for instance, as it is for many of us, physical exercise and diet may be very helpful.

An obvious concern that is most overlooked is forgetting to take the medication or overlooking the need for refills at the pharmacy. My wife, Donna, helps me with refilling prescriptions - that has been enormously helpful. After taking them, I turn my drinking glass upside down, or check for water in it, to help me determine if I've taken the medications. Other individuals use pill holders. Forgetting to take medications, over time, can still be very problematic.

Beyond all the problems for individuals who take responsibility for their own mental health, there is still one more, little realized, yet potentially serious difficulty; the interaction between mental health and other physical health issues. Individuals with mental health concerns often have the same physical health problems as most other people. My difficulties with physical health include a bout with salmonella. When I was so ill that I was hospitalized, my body eventually purged all the salmonella poison out of its system along with the medications. I was cured of food poisoning, but stricken with mental illness.

THE PROMISE OF LONG TERM RECOVERY

These examples and overall discussion are meant to demonstrate how difficult any given situation can be when medications are involved. There is so much information about medications that it is impossible to explain the entire issue, especially when opinions are so divergent on the whole range of concerns associated with them. Again, medications are not "magic beans" that make life easy for individuals with bipolar disorder.

It is nearly impossible to explain the level of patience, forbearance, and perseverance needed to live a fulfilling life for those of us who live with the illness every day. Nor is it possible to describe the courage required to live with the realization that we are so fundamentally different from others. The challenges and uncertainties are daunting at times; but medication, I believe, can be a crucial element in long term recovery that makes the journey both possible and worthwhile.

3. 10 Observations about Bipolar Disorder

1. Bipolar Disorder Defined

Some members of society believe mental illnesses are caused by lack of faith, the inability to handle stress, and character flaws. This attitude may even exist within the individual because of societal beliefs. The illness is not the individual's fault, but it is their responsibility to manage. So much time is often spent on stressing the responsibility, it begins to feel like it *is* our fault. Then, the illness begins to feel like a punishment and humiliation. This becomes a real problem.

Scientific truth explains bipolar disorder as a *biological* brain disorder with psychological symptoms. There is no definitive diagnosis or cure.

Bipolar disorder is diagnosed by observing a collection of symptoms, genetics, and identifying how medications affect other physical illnesses. For example, tegretol is frequently used for both epilepsy and bipolar disorder.

2. Personal Attitude Changes

Because acceptance of a bipolar disorder diagnosis requires a major attitude change, it is something that usually can't be embraced immediately. Far less complicated ideas, like voting for a political candidate, may require a number of speeches over a considerable length of time. Yet, individuals with a mental illness are often required to accept a major mental illness, hastily and entirely. This can deeply affect the individual's self-esteem, identity, and even spirituality.

Many famous people, past and present have been required to accept and manage their bipolar disorder. This can often promote acceptance and enhance self-esteem.

[See Chapter below: *Famous People with Bipolar Disorder*]

3. Onset Effects for Young Adults

Often, an individual's first experience with bipolar disorder occurs during young

adulthood. This is a time when independence and self-discovery are very important. Individuals are away from home, actively pursuing their own interests. Then, usually without warning, they're burdened with a mental illness, living at home, and have more supervision than ever. As more realistic goals are sought, it feels like the individual's life is being stolen.

A diagnosis of bipolar disorder may be a life changing experience, but it also provides unique opportunities to explore the mind and emotions, enhance creativity, and overcome troubling states like depression.

A bipolar diagnosis can be very challenging and life is long. Taking time to manage the illness now brings future benefits such as complex, useful coping strategies.

4. Importance of Medications

Medications may make everything else possible, but guarantee nothing. They simply give us the *chance* to lead productive lives. Individuals still face stigma, discrimination, and other obstacles associated with our illness. Medications are not "silver bullets" that manage the illness entirely. Self-effort is extraordinarily important.

To avoid frustration, humiliation, and the lack of cooperation that follows, individuals need to be acknowledged for their own self-effort and perseverance.

5. Medications : Weight Gain

A major problem associated with bipolar disorder medications is weight gain. This common side effect also creates health concerns and self-esteem issues. Diabetes and hypertension are concerns over time. Gaining thirty pounds in a couple of months is difficult to bear. Once the medications are discontinued, sometimes the weight comes right back off again, and so does the risk of a relapse.

Physical exercise, diet, and sleep can help manage weight gain to some degree. For a lot of us, even with these good habits, weight gain is still troublesome.

However, it is also true that for most of us, the illness is much worse. It's dangerous, depressing, and isolating.

6. Medications : Quality of Life

For some individuals, medication doesn't improve their quality of life. Either they continue to relapse, can't find steady employment, or lack any genuine sense of purpose. The medication has been promised to bring relief, but it has done little to help.

If the medications aren't working, maybe they're not the right ones.

There are other possible reasons for not feeling better, such as absence of routines and lack of exercise.

Volunteer jobs provide excellent ways to fill the day with purpose and routine. They can also become useful references for the future.

7. Medications : Some Issues

Some fairly common, but less identified, problems with medications include initial bad experiences, misunderstanding of the recurrence of bipolar disorder, and the difficulty in treating the illness in some individuals.

Some individuals are reluctant to stay on medications because they were either traumatized by a misdiagnosis or were adversely affected by a medication.

Some see bipolar disorder as a kind of flu that will not recur.

Sadly, there are still other individuals that don't receive substantive help by any medications currently on the market.

8. Concentration, Stability and Calmness

The idea that medications have a negative impact on self-expression, creativity, and spirituality is certainly true for some; for others medications enhance these activities because they facilitate concentration, stability, and calmness. It is then more likely that daily life and relationships remain more stable and predictable. This allows for the creative person to have one "foot on the ground and one foot in the sky".

9. Medications : Refusal and Relapse

If a relapse occurs because of medication refusal, individuals could unexpectedly be hospitalized anywhere, even in another state. Since mental health professionals in these new settings aren't familiar with the individual's diagnosis, it makes treatment more difficult. Employment positions and essential relationships may be lost, requiring us to "start from scratch".

10. Social Judgements and Personal Denial

To a casual observer, the idea that individuals with bipolar disorder are unwilling to take their medications seems irresponsible and even absurd. With no frame of reference, the observer doesn't realize that they and society are actually part of the cause for this attitude.

If individuals don't accept or identify with a bipolar disorder, then in their mind, they don't have the illness. This in turn means they don't have to accept the stigma, discrimination, humiliation, and the other burdens that go with it.

This includes concerns about jobs, relationships, insurance, and other important life problems. Everyone wants to "fix" us. Society could help by actually accepting us and "fixing" <u>their</u> attitudes.

4. Coping Strategies: Developing Lines of Defense

Coping skills are an integral part of the recovery process. These strategies are the one element of long term recovery that individuals with bipolar disorder can discover on their own and develop according to their own specific needs. Because of their importance as acquired skills, these strategies can also serve as uniquely individual contributions to overall recovery.

While coping skills are sometimes introduced by professionals, they are really techniques that must be learned and practiced routinely, so they become increasingly useful in times of stress, and when symptoms threaten to take hold. Taken together, coping skills form a kind of defense system providing important opportunities to manage thoughts and feelings before they overwhelm. Coping skills can help reduce the frequency of hospital stays and greatly improve an individual's quality of life.

Coping strategies are a number of skills, developed over time, which address specific symptoms unique to an individual. Some examples of symptoms include racing thoughts, anxiety, and insomnia. When these symptoms appear, the idea is to employ various coping strategies to neutralize or minimize the symptoms' effects.

For me; for example, when I have racing thoughts, I meditate; for anxiety, I jog. For insomnia, I use visualization techniques. The point is that when stress and symptoms arise, I employ specific tools to deal with their impact. Such strategies can be learned and practiced repeatedly when stress and symptoms are not present. In that way, the skills are readily accessible when difficult situations actually do arise.

Creating and developing these effective lines of defense sometimes takes years. They are based on trial and error and their benefits are specific to the individual. Most individuals' preferences and lifestyles vary greatly; these differences can be essential factors in choosing and practicing specific coping skills. If these skills are to be useful in a wide variety of settings, they must also be practical. For example, if an individual's one main coping skill is swimming, and there is no pool or lake around, this strategy, though valuable, cannot be relied on as the only tool for combating symptoms, stress, and medication side effects.

So, how are coping skills discovered and developed into useful techniques? Individuals can begin with activities they already do. For example, hot showers and long baths are both surprisingly helpful in relieving stress and altering moods. For me, cleaning the house, gardening, and snow shoveling almost always help me let go of anxious thoughts and misdirected nervous energy. These pursuits also help fill my day with meaningful activities and keep boredom and loneliness from filling my mind with anxious worries. This idea of filling the day with activities is one of the most important coping strategies, and can be defined, in general terms, as creating routines.

Of all the presentations I have heard involving long term recovery, the establishing of detailed routines is almost always credited as an important source of assistance. A meaningful plan for the day is often a good way to both gain self-confidence and feel a sense of accomplishment. Routines continually keep the mind engaged, so it is not left to conjure up restless thoughts and anxious feelings. Instead of simply letting the day just "happen", so nothing accomplished until late afternoon – when individuals then remember things they could have done – a specific routine begins the day with meaningful activity. The day then progresses with intention and the mind is positively engaged. Sitting around watching TV or listening to music creates the illusion of activity; but being passive activities, neither the body nor the mind is actively involved. It requires time and patience to develop a series of activities to create a daily routine; but it can be a powerful way to help prolong a successful recovery.

The lack of useful routines can lead to boredom and isolation. These in themselves can lead to mental discord – they can even threaten recovery itself. When symptoms manifest because of boredom and loneliness, medications are sometimes changed and experimented with even though they aren't necessarily the real source of the distress.

Even with exactly the right medicines; boredom, loneliness, and environmental changes may be the cause of symptoms. The truth is medications can be difficult to integrate into our brain chemistry. Once the medications are working, routines and coping skills may be needed to fill in the gap between what the medications can accomplish, and what the individual's own self-effort can achieve. Although individuals with mental illnesses are rarely given credit for their own self-effort, their perseverance is just as important as the medications themselves. This determination, for me and many others, has been a very crucial reason for our long term recoveries.

Coping skills can be described as assisting individuals with bipolar disorder to "get inside our own heads," so we can actively manage our thoughts and feelings ourselves.

<u>They allow us to:</u>
    slow down our thoughts,
    redirect nervous energy, and
    channel our emotions in a positive way.

It is true that medication and counseling help, yet they are indirect and not under our immediate control. Medication for example, acts almost independently and individuals can "work with them", but can't literally control them.

Talk therapies provide important ideas and guidance, but cannot literally control the random wanderings of the mind and the infinite number of thoughts that can suddenly arise when no one else is around.

Slowing Down Thoughts

So, to slow down thoughts and the thinking process generally, one must manage thoughts directly. This can be done in a variety of ways. For me, one important skill I've practiced for a very long time is meditation. Before learning this skill, I was repeatedly relapsing because of my inability to stop my mind from churning out painful memories of the past and expectations about the future. All day long, I was constantly inundated by these unwanted thoughts and emotions, with no way to get rid of them or redirect them.

However, when I began meditating for only twenty minutes a day, my mind slowed down long enough that I could begin to recognize these thought forms and categorize them. Before long, the categories included past, present, and future time, as well as random imaginative thinking. This helped me understand my problems while simultaneously slowing down the thinking process.

I ignored this valuable coping strategy for years. I ridiculed the entire concept, considering the practice absurd. It was only after repeated hospitalizations and when everything else had failed, that, in utter desperation, I finally turned to meditation. The medication and counseling were working, but they couldn't eliminate the symptoms entirely. This difficult situation required me to learn effective coping skills like meditation to manage my own specific needs.

There are examples of meditation practice being utilized in less critical situations pointing to its effectiveness. For instance, parents sometimes advise their children to "slow down, take a deep breath, and count to ten". This is essentially meditation. The purpose of this advice is to slow down the mind and body, so the child can calm down and center. The mind is tied to the breath. The slower the breathing becomes, the slower the mind functions.

Meditation has some very useful, unexpected benefits for managing thoughts and moods. For instance, it aids in concentration because it focuses attention and energy; it can, at times, transcend the thinking process. This also expands conscious awareness promoting emotional and spiritual growth. I must emphasize, what it *hasn't* done for me – cure my bipolar disorder or allow me to stop taking medications. Nevertheless, the meditative coping skill continues to provide a valuable strategy I can use to manage symptoms.

Redirecting Nervous Energy

In addition to managing thoughts, another difficult problem is the redirecting of nervous energy. For many of us, it is fair to say that if our energy is not directed in productive ways, it will soon become misdirected and take the form of worry and anxiety. In other words, sitting idle for long periods of time rarely solves any problems. The lack of physical activity becomes highly problematic. This tendency for the mind to turn to thoughts of fear and nervousness is a problem for everyone to some degree. For those of us struggling with stress and symptom management, it presents a serious risk to our long term recovery.

For generalized nervous energy, physical exercise is an effective coping strategy. This skill can be uniquely individual, yet very powerful; exercise seems to transform listlessness and lethargy into constructive energy, temporarily freeing the individual from the grip of anxiety and depression. This practice cannot be overemphasized. Physical exercise can help elevate our mood, raise our level of self-esteem, and fend off boredom. It is not a cure in itself, but it definitely offers relief.

The problem is following through with exercising. The most important thing to consider is which specific form of exercise provides relief in managing symptoms. If some specific exercise works, then it could become part of a daily/weekly routine. This activity could develop with patience and practice.

For me, the two most important times to exercise are when I'm feeling depressed and thoughts become anxious, and when my body is wound up and affecting my peace of mind. A lot of times I'm not "in the mood" to exercise, but I do it anyway without thinking much about it.

Channeling Emotions

Another specific area where coping skills can be very helpful is when emotions are the source of our difficulties. Our diagnosis indicates we experience a wide range of emotions that are sometimes difficult to bear. They are detrimental to our employment situations and relationships generally.

Emotions like anger can be very inappropriate in the work place and can adversely affect other areas of our life including friendships and family relationships. There are times when we feel compelled to express our thoughts and feelings, even though they would best be expressed in other places and in other ways. Since counselors and good friends aren't always available, coping strategies that help ease frustration, anger, and anxiety can help redirect, channel, and eventually dissipate these potentially disruptive emotions. Activities like journaling, creative writing, listening music, singing, painting, drawing and photography can help individuals facilitate self-expression and provide a sense of closure while redirecting emotions toward positive experiences.

To be fair, there are many situations in which anger and frustration are justified due to discrimination and stigma, but expressing them can make things worse. For me, my association with NAMI (The National Alliance on Mental Illness) has given me the chance to give presentations and to make and keep friends. Chipmunka Publishing (self-publishing) has given me the opportunity to express myself in creative writing projects. Anger and depression are on-going problems for me; but with the help of creative outlets, they are far less of a challenge now.

Benefits of Coping Strategies

There are many important benefits to coping strategies that go far beyond slowing the mind and redirecting anxious energy. Probably the most important advantage of coping skills is their effectiveness in keeping individuals out of emergency rooms when symptoms and stress begin to take over. Because of the self-knowledge involved in acquiring these skills, mental difficulties can often be identified and dealt with while the crisis is still developing, before it really takes hold. This promotes a sense of self-confidence in our ability to manage potentially difficult predicaments while also sparing us from the mental and financial burdens associated with hospitalizations. It reinforces both the need and the effectiveness of the coping skills we possess.

These strategies can be generalized into other areas of life that are really beneficial. One of the most obvious is physical exercise. This activity promotes physical health, improves self-esteem and can lead to opportunities for socializing. As a part of an overall strategy, exercise is certainly one of the most practical and helpful coping skill.

Strategy about Sleep

Another helpful strategy is developing a sleep routine, which can be indispensable for many individuals with bipolar disorder. Lack of sleep or an irregular sleep pattern can be the single most serious explanation for irritability and interpersonal problems. Even the realization that we are tired, doesn't guarantee we'll be able to control our emotions, unless we remain quiet during these times.

The sleeping pattern, with regular bedtime and wake-up times, helps insure that insomnia doesn't lead to racing thoughts and anxiety. This rhythm of sleeping and waking is somewhat rigid and hardly promotes spontaneity, but it is yet another, sacrifice many individuals with mental illness are required to make order to stay healthy.

Fortunately, the self-discipline required to follow a specific sleep schedule, also generalizes into other activities which can lead to increased self-effort and patience. This, in turn, creates an attitude of resilience, one of the most important coping skills of all. These experiences provide structure and help minimize uncertainty.

Strategy about Positive Character Qualities

These attitudes and habits are a part of a wide range of coping strategies that represent a shift in perspective about how individuals with mental illness manage their lives. For instance, individuals with bipolar disorder almost always have at least some pent up anger, fear, and desire for justice. These feelings are genuine, based on real experiences. Yet, in order to move forward in the spirit of resilience and adaptability, these feelings and memories that sometimes poison our lives must be dealt with, (perhaps in counseling), and then left behind. This attitude can be difficult to develop, yet allows us to move freely into the present without all the "baggage" we have carried for so long.

The point is that positive character qualities are very valuable coping strategies when experiences and situations become troubling. My problems with pride, anger, and impatience, for example, still affect my relationships and peace of mind; however, gratitude and humility have helped overcome my negativity, allowing for alternate responses. Instead of simply reacting angrily mentally or verbally, there is now a "space" where I choose to control myself and so better adapt to changing situations.

Strategy for Vivid Memories About Episodes

Another concept that has generalized into a coping technique for me was suggested by a psychiatrist. Most individuals with bipolar disorder have vivid memories of their psychotic episode experiences. They realize psychotic thoughts often come and go long after the "psychotic breaks" have passed. These situations can be degrading and unnerving.

When I discussed these concerns with my psychiatrist, he had a helpful suggestion. He explained with an analogy. He said that if one foot begins to slide away from the other, just gently slide it back. This simple idea has turned out to be very effective because it took the fear out of these thoughts whenever they would arise. This simple technique was also easily applicable for other unwanted thoughts that inevitably bubble up in my mind.

Strategy for Introversion

Another coping suggestion addresses the problems of introversion so often affecting those of us with a mental illness. At times, our thoughts and feelings are so unruly we tend to isolate ourselves from others, for understandable reasons. This isolation is not caused by selfishness or indifference. It is because we are constantly monitoring and managing symptoms that take precedent during these times. Sometimes we isolate ourselves because we have had a prior lack of success in relationships and/or there are few activities that genuinely interest us.

Many of the problematic thoughts and emotions associated with bipolar disorder can lead to uncertainty when it comes to our responses to those around us. It can be extraordinarily challenging to understand the verbal and nonverbal behavior of ourselves and others when symptoms arise. The creation of specific ways to handle these difficult situations can sometimes make the difference between sustaining a long term recovery or relapsing.

One of the most obvious, yet most frightening, solutions to this isolation is to metaphorically "dive in". Introversion is generally unadvisable long term. This strategy helps an individual test their ideas; and after some success in a positive environment, they will will find a measure of hope, purpose, and self-confidence.

Fears and anxieties may decrease when individuals become less preoccupied with their own thoughts and emotions. By joining others, we "take a vacation from ourselves" which may help redirect our attention. This introversion also produces flings of loneliness, boredom, and anxiety. This state of mind is rarely advisable as a long term coping technique. Involvement with activities that are genuinely interesting can be instrumental in the process of recovery. Everyone is motivated by something. When that something is discovered, it is a good place to start.

Strategy for Relaxation

A coping technique that is frequently overlooked is listening to music to relax and inspire. Since ancient times music has been an integral part of society. Today, it is available in many forms

Since the aim of almost all musical composition is to create certain moods within the listener, it follows that music can help relieve anxiety, help lift depressive moods, and even enhance creativity. The type of music is based on individual taste – new age, classical, blue grass, etc. Many kinds of music may be useful in improving an individual's mood especially when it is played in order to enrich ongoing creative and social activities.

The converse is also true. Music that is meant to create a feeling of melancholy or even despair may also affect thoughts and feelings. When I was young, for example, I sometimes listened to depressing songs repeatedly, and this inevitably led to withdrawal and depression.

This paradox about music is important to understand. Individuals can unwittingly be exposed to any type of music for extended periods of time with unanticipated results. Once individuals with bipolar disorder identify what kinds of music affect them and in what ways; music can be part of their defense system - an added coping tool. It can serve as a source of comfort in the form of relaxation or as a backdrop for creative inspiration.

Famous People with Bipolar Disorder

For me, and for many other individuals, the study of famous people in history who have struggled with bipolar disorder, provides the greatest sense of hope. By studying the lives of famous men and women who have been stricken with a mental illness, many of us find courage and inspiration. [See the Chapter titled: *Famous People with Bipolar Disorder*]

We learn to overcome society's discrimination and distrust by prevailing over their ignorance with our own sense of dignity and self-worth. Mental illness has been so condemned throughout history that it often takes a little digging to discover the deep effect these illnesses and had on these historical figures and how they managed to excel anyway. Reading about their lives can provide a way to cope with bipolar disorder and the stigma still associated with it. Two famous people, Abraham Lincoln and Francis of Assisi, are good examples.

Abraham Lincoln sometimes had serious bouts of what can only be described as clinical depression. As a young man, when his girlfriend died, he was found in the woods with a rifle. His friends kept him in a "safe house" until his desperate mood passed. Later, when he was president, he never carried a gun because he was afraid he'd use it on himself. However, not surprisingly, some historians have argued that Lincoln's depression eventually made him a stronger leader.

Another towering figure who was considered mentally ill for part of his life was the Roman Catholic Saint Francis of Assisi. During his spiritual transformation, his mind was subject to extreme mood swings and his behavior was considered to be those of a "madman". Once he even tossed his father's possessions out on to the street giving them all away. Shortly afterward, he took off his clothes in front of the whole town. These mental states were transitory; however, they make the point that individuals with a mental illness can overcome and succeed despite their daunting challenges. Furthermore, by learning about famous people, individuals with bipolar disorder can draw inspiration and find reassurances even when society is cruel or indifferent.

Two areas in which coping skills are exceedingly important are employment and relationships. In these situations, a combination of coping strategies, good judgment, and common sense are required to be successful.

The first strategy involves becoming a good actor. As almost all of us discover, eventually we must hide our illness. Most people are not educated about mental challenges; so they rely on stereotypes to try and understand. Because of this, we essentially lead a double life. Many people are unwilling to accept us if we have a mental illness.

Strategies about Employment

This is most obvious when it applies to employment. Laws against discrimination when it comes to individuals with mental illnesses are meaningless. I have never found employment by telling the truth, nor have I found work if perspective employers have found out my "secret" through exhaustive background checks.

In light of this sad truth, a couple of things are helpful to know. On resumes and applications, it is important to leave out any mental illness experiences. They are almost always deal breakers. On applications, for instance, writing down that one was in a state mental health facility or in a halfway house hardly seems prudent. Instead, filling in the time with something else such as a "my relative was ill, so I took some time off" seems like a better strategy. It's not a question of being honest; it's a question of economic survival. Society wants it both ways. They won't hire us, but they want us to work. By doing an exceptional job after being hired, individuals can justify their actions to themselves if they feel uncomfortable with deception. Sometimes the ends *do* justify the means.

Employment is another area where coping skills become very valuable. The urge at an employment interview is to tell the truth, clear the air, and take the pressure off our shoulders. The problem is the ultimate goal is sacrificed. The truth almost always frightens people, at least initially; then the interview either ends suspiciously, or it begins to resemble a therapy session. A support system is the perfect way to deal with the pressure. Over time this group, in whatever form it takes, can help in these critical situations.

This attitude is best maintained throughout an employment experience. It is a great temptation for individuals to gossip about others even in seemingly harmless ways. Unfortunately, coworkers, after they know about an individual's mental health issues, may begin to watch for symptoms. This can lead to feelings of anger and betrayal. Developing a reliable and empathetic support system away from work is a good strategy, so our needs are met. It takes self-control, patience, and self-confidence to hold back from the authentic desire to tell the truth. Fortunately, these positive attitudes protect us from the ignorance of others.

Strategies about Relationships

The importance of a support system helps immensely with this secret life we are required to maintain. Friends, family, mental health professionals, and organizations can give us the understanding and freedom we need to drop the mask. Ironically, individuals with a mental illness have two jobs. In a very real sense, staying healthy is a full time job in itself. At times, when symptoms and stress manifest, it becomes the most pressing problem in our lives, eclipsing all else, including employment and relationships. Support groups are essential in helping us juggle both the problems of employment and the secret challenges of our illness.

Finally, relationships can be very valuable but sometimes problematic for individuals with bipolar disorder. For me, one of my biggest challenges involves consistently misinterpreting conversations and situations occurring in the course of the day. I misunderstand what people say because I confuse the message and the tone. I assume the person is angry or disappointed with me. I agonize whether I said "the right thing" to the other person. I tend to misread nonverbal behavior as negative. Fortunately, my wife, Donna, often helps me better understand these situations when they come up.

This misinterpretation of people and events can be especially troubling when symptoms like depression, hunger, sleeplessness, and mistrust begin to appear. Irritability, impatience, and the desire to "finish" things can be very difficult to control when working and talking with others. These negative thoughts can create unrealistic expectations leading to frustration and anger. It is only the most durable relationships that survive when an individual with bipolar disorder loses control. Hurtful words can be very difficult to forgive and forget.

A final note about relationships that is exceedingly difficult for individuals with mental illness. Almost everyone in our culture drinks alcohol. It is a problem for us because it can lead to depression and sometimes triggering a manic episode. Alcohol is served almost everywhere, for almost any reason - it can be difficult to resist. I try to remember that most people use alcohol as their own coping mechanism. This reinforces my own belief that individuals with mental illnesses are often stronger in will power than most of the rest of society.

Knowledge <u>Is</u> Power

It is important to note the relevance of the concept that "knowledge is power". Mental health professionals, relatives, and friends can often provide suggestions and support; but most of us confronted with a major mental illness have to figure out the way forward alone at times. If indeed we are attempting to sustain a long term recovery; self-effort, perseverance, and self-knowledge are indispensable.

It is true that others can be very helpful, even essential. But, they can't take the journey for us. The more individuals educate themselves about bipolar disorder and explore the possible coping strategies available, the greater the likelihood of success. This search for answers also gives the feeling of relief and empowerment once these coping skills begin to evolve.

The development and regular use of these strategies can make the difference, in time, between living a life of hope and purpose, or simply "treading water" and "just hanging on".

5. 10 Valuable Coping Strategies

To Enhance Long Term Recovery....

The following inventory of coping strategies can be employed as important "lines of defense". They are useful in the management of thoughts, feelings, and moods. These skills, when practiced consistently, can help limit the intensity and duration of intrusive symptoms while promoting self-confidence, self-discipline, and perseverance. I have used these successfully.

Coping skills are intended to be used together. By putting a few big things together with many little things, long term recovery gradually gains momentum. They gradually replace the old destructive habits like alcohol, drugs, and problematic attitudes and behaviors.

1. Exercise

Regular physical exercise can help manage stress and redirect nervous energy. It promotes a feeling of being "grounded," so that thoughts and feelings are more focused. Physical exercise addresses medication side effects like weight gain and lethargy. Some examples of physical exercise include: walking, hiking, jogging, swimming, biking, camping, mall walking, work outs on gym equipment, yoga, martial arts, tai chi, and recorded exercise routines.

2. Meditation / Relaxation

Coping skills such as meditation and other relaxation techniques can be a valuable part of any effective defense system, when symptoms become so problematic that hospitalizations threaten a long term recovery. Sometimes, the difference between being admitted to the hospital and feeling emotionally secure is the regular practice of relaxation techniques, that continually help to ease stress, slow down racing thoughts and quiet troubling emotions.

[See Chapter: *A Simple Meditation to Relax the Mind and Body*]

3. Routines / Activities

Specific daily routines are essential for any long term recovery. Remain active all day, every day. Some approaches include making lists of chores and other activities. This creates a sense of purpose and engages the mind, so it doesn't manufacture worry, loneliness, and boredom. Since stress is often a problem, procrastination is an attitude to overcome. It simply adds to all the other anxiety and worry we already carry around. Crossing off each item on the list as it is completed provides a sense of satisfaction and completion. At the end of the day review the list and remember how you felt as each task was completed. Examples of routines and chores include: washing the dishes, doing the laundry, shopping for food, housework (vacuuming, cleaning tables and counters, toilets and showers, dusting, sweeping the floors), mowing the grass, weeding the garden.

Volunteering can help fill the day with meaningful activities and offer a possible job reference for the future. Other social activities can also serve as coping strategies that help promote socialization and long term recovery.

- Volunteer ideas include: churches, social service organizations, food pantry, resale shops, and hospitals.

- Some social activities are: museum trips, window shopping, coffee klatches, planned group exercises, flea market browsing, Second hand store browsing (also a good place for bargain prices) and garage sales.

4. Regular Sleeping Patterns

A regular sleep schedule helps insure a good night's rest. Irritability and anxiety can seem like symptoms of a mental illness when they are actually symptoms of insomnia or being tired. A daily bath or shower can be a surprisingly effective way to temporarily drain away anxiety, fear, and worry.

5. Positive Attitudes

Positive attitudes can be learned and practiced. They can be useful in a variety of personal and social settings. By avoiding extremes in emotions like "riding out feelings to the end," the individual can foster improved moods which can be more conducive to long term recovery. Understanding that bipolar disorder isn't our fault helps build self-confidence in our interactions with others and allows guilt to dissolve.

6. Forgiveness

Learning to forgive the many injustices we have experienced allows us to live in the present instead of brooding over angry memories and painful humiliation. By practicing forgiveness the sharpness of such experiences can fade with time. We have enough work in managing day-to-day life without carrying the poor choices made by others as well.

7. Medications

When medications are taken for a sufficient length of time, they can provide the stability to discover and develop appropriate coping skills. They become powerful allies when needed. Starting over with medications repeatedly, makes it more difficult to learn and practice these strategies. *The root cause of bipolar disorder is a physiological brain disorder.* Even with the best coping skills, the illness will probably remain.

8. Counseling / Support Systems

Bipolar disorder requires a complex strategy to manage effectively, so counselors and other support systems are essential. Due to our illness and society's stigma, navigating the employment, health, and educational systems can be overwhelming. Counselors and other support personnel have experience dealing with these institutions, and may be enormously helpful.

To understand bipolar disorder, we must identify what it is, how it affects us, and how it affects our relationships. These can be difficult to sort out alone.

The enemies of loneliness and boredom can be so unbearable that they can drain us of every joy. Sometimes a good support system can be very helpful in combating these difficult states of mind.

9. Self-Knowledge

One of the most valuable coping strategies is self-knowledge. Learning about bipolar disorder and continually observing how the illness affects the body and mind can be a rewarding and reassuring practice that helps keep a long term recovery on track.

10. Creativity

All kinds of creative endeavors can be exceedingly productive coping strategies because, they not only provide an outlet for managing symptoms, but they also produce the opportunity for genuine artistic expression. Some creative activities are: drawing, painting, singing, dancing, playing a musical instrument, writing (books, poetry, journals), gardening, tai chi and martial arts

6. Psychology: Limitations and Benefits

This chapter describes a number of the psychological symptoms associated with bipolar disorder and offers some explanations for the unusual thoughts and feelings often experienced by individuals struggling with this illness.

It includes some rather unique features of the diagnosis that may be useful for families, mental health professionals and, especially for individuals. By paying close attention, it is my belief that some common ideas and behaviors can be discovered that are often misunderstood or ignored. Recognizing these common symptoms may also provide some important clues about the nature and severity of the illness itself.

There are also some unorthodox interpretations of bipolar disorder that are beyond the realm of most conventional forms of psychotherapy.

I believe that by identifying some of these causes and symptoms, mental health professionals can better understand the motivation and behavior of the individuals they serve and so help them to get their legitimate needs met. In turn, these individuals might have a better chance of sustaining a long term recovery.

These are not meant to minimize the importance of medication and counseling. These two important aspects of treatment are vital – we ignore them at our peril.

One significant way to help individuals with bipolar disorder find their way involves facilitating their genuine desire for change. On one level, the illness represents an effort to break out of a restrictive form of consciousness and seek a more expansive way of being. Sometimes, the struggling individual is searching for a radically new way of finding fulfillment in life. This psychological crisis is often overwhelming and intense, and may even be unintelligible to the individuals themselves.

It is sometimes a driving force that helps triggering the onset and development of the illness.

What I'm suggesting is that psychology, although indispensable, doesn't provide <u>all</u> the answers for many of us struggling with a mental illness, who are desperately trying to evolve. I think the basic problem is psychological / medical [the Standard Model] treatments are based almost exclusively on the mind and body. The scientific view often sees these as the sum total of existence, that which can be objectively identified. This approach does lead to many important therapies and medicines, but it doesn't always analyze symptoms in a comprehensive way.

In general, the Standard Model describes the individual with bipolar disorder as being ill and in need of treatment, certainly accurate. The mental health professional's task becomes: correctly diagnosing, stabilizing the individual using medications, counseling, and support.

As the crisis passes, the hope of recovery dawns; the promise of *long term recovery* begins to take shape. As the right combinations of medications are discovered, counseling becomes more comprehensive. This kind of therapy usually includes the individual regaining self-esteem and self-confidence.

Finally, as individuals restore their identity, the recovery process brings the them "back to their old selves," so to speak. Then the separate self is firmly back in control allowing them to get on with life. Or can they?

What if the Standard Model is incomplete? Suppose there are explanations for symptoms that include ideas not usually considered during the treatment process?

For instance, obsessive and delusional thoughts about God are usually considered manifestations of the illness, and are described as symptoms of "religiosity". This concept is generally defined as an unhealthy fixation on God. It is viewed as a way for individuals to avoid facing their problems.

Yet, it seems very reasonable that individuals who are seriously mentally ill *would* turn to God for help. Many people with a major physical illness turn to God for comfort and healing. Just because the basic human need may be distorted by delusional thinking and unstable behavior doesn't nullify the basic principle that the individual is seeking answers.

The real crux of the problem with the Standard Model is that it doesn't go deep enough. It is extremely useful for a wide variety of situations, but it sees the "mind itself as the true source of being. The mind is assumed to create and sustain the separate, individual self as the ultimate state of existence.

The following model attempts to more clearly explain the distinctions between the psychological approach to a crisis and a more spiritual orientation.

Mental Illness as a Psychological Crisis – The Model of Treatment

Stage 1: The illness manifests: individuals experience uncontrolled mood swings; sometimes accompanied by racing thoughts, inability to sleep, delusional thinking, etc.

Stage 2: Efforts are made to heal the mind with medication, counseling, and self-effort.

Stage 3: Self effort and self-confidence are encouraged so as to restore the individual to their separate identity.

Stage 4: Individuals are assisted in supporting their separate individual identity.

Stage 5: They gradually begin to fully participate in life again.

I was deeply immersed in this approach to recovery for many years. It provided a final stage of therapy that was very helpful, to a point. It limited my development to a restoration of the individual self. Because the process ended at Stage 5, it failed to address my deeper concerns, so I continually fell back into illness at Stage 1.

When I was finally helped to expand my approach, my mental health gradually improved. Instead of consistently relapsing back into Stage 1 of the psychological model, I was able to move into a more spiritual orientation that began where the psychological model ended.

- I began to understand that the "separate self" is limiting.

- I began to relinquish various thoughts and desires through meditation and life-style changes.

- I realized the "separate self" doesn't need to be supreme at all times.

- It became clear the "separate self" was less important than I once believed.

- An intuitive awareness emerged with deeper insight and expansion of consciousness.

Once these additional steps were added to my treatment, my progress was steady, relapses were very infrequent. Over a number a years, my long term recovery took hold, and I began to experience a much improved quality of life.

Finding the right medications and my willingness to take them early on would have certainly accelerated my recovery. It is also true that at no time were my genuine metaphysical concerns addressed. Although I'm certain some approaches to therapy now include these underlying spiritual impulses, I never personally experienced them as an integral part of any psychological model program.

For individuals who continue to relapse, the strategy of leading them back to some "former self" may be problematic. It is, after all, that "former self" that was not very functional. This failure to recover sometimes occurs even with effective medications because, I believe, the basic need for meaningful change is left unfulfilled. Individuals become trapped in the Standard Model.

Sadly, there are few, if any, specific scientific theories that recognize a form of consciousness beyond the "mind" or "separate self". So individuals with bipolar disorder often struggle to understand thoughts, feelings, and behaviors that are usually unrecognizable to others. One of the main reasons for adding the spiritual segment to the Standard Model is to explain the problem of relapse, and its relationship to a closed system. Since spiritual principles ultimately go beyond personal thoughts and emotions, the mind itself is not always the only source of concern.

The mind is a vast network of interwoven thoughts, emotions (feelings), memories, tendencies, desires, sensations, etc. that collectively create the "separate self". It is like a ball of yarn created by collecting individual colored strands accumulated over many years. Studying the huge ball, it would appear to have a core or center. Yet, methodically unravelling it strand by strand would ultimately reveal there is no center at all. Nothing is left.

That "nothing" is actually something. It is consciousness devoid of contents like thoughts and emotions. It may be called intuition and spirit. Some have suggested this intuitive consciousness allows for unlimited growth and expansion.

In the Standard Model, I almost never received useful information about spiritual development. When I was mentally ill seeking spiritual experiences, I fell into delusional thinking, reached dead ends, and engaged in risky behavior. With no inner compass, my concept of God being a "guy in the sky" remained intact. My addictive personality surrendered my intelligence until I was emotionally crippled. My inability to make independent decisions gradually paralyzed my mind, so that even mundane choices were difficult. For example, "Does God want me to buy the chocolate donut or the cream filled donut?" This kind of orientation regarding spiritual development was constrictive and unhealthy.

Nevertheless, psychological concepts have been enormously helpful for me. They have required me to examine my motives, memories, and conditioning - it has been indispensable. To re-emphasize: _psychological theories and therapies are crucial in the treatment of mental illness._

Counseling

For most , when we ignore our thoughts and feelings, they surface in unexpected, and some times unpleasant ways. The mind will not be forgotten or slighted; especially when an individual attempts to awaken spiritual experiences. Without a proper understanding of the deeper recesses of the mind, it can be difficult to find the way. If these attempts to seek God are misguided, they can lead to "crash landings". Unfortunately, delusional thinking sometimes has the vibrant feel of a genuine spiritual experience, self-knowledge is very important

[See Chapter: _10 Valuable Coping Strategies_]

Consequently, counseling has been essential for my long term recovery. The expansion of awareness that attempts to understand the mind is a necessarily long and difficult process.

There are some less philosophical reasons for counseling for those struggling with bipolar disorder. For many of us to successfully manage our illness, we must understand its effects in at least three important situations.

General Knowledge

We must understand what the illness is in general terms. This includes its overall definition as a biological brain disorder with radical mood swings and a delusional component sometimes associated with it. Many times other symptoms such as suicidal thoughts are connected with it.

Personal Understanding

We need to understand how the illness affects us personally. Despite understanding an overall, general explanation about bipolar disorder, every individual needs to understand their unique symptoms.

Everyone has a different brain chemistry that is affected differently by medications.

Different groups of symptoms are often unique to specific individuals making the diagnosis and management of the illness extremely subjective.

Counseling is very useful in identifying these specific symptoms and helping individuals recognize them.

Social Impacts

The illness must be seen in terms of its impact on social networks and relationships. The importance of realizing how we interact with those around us can't be overstated especially when employment, family, and friendships are at risk. Very often an individual's moods and perceptions influence the interpretations of situations.

The motives and attitudes of others can easily be misunderstood when symptoms are affecting our judgment. Without some awareness and acceptance of this limitation, we "wander around in the dark", sabotaging our relationships with others who we want and need in our lives.

As if these reasons for counseling weren't enough, there is an even more compelling reason generally overlooked by society. Due to our bipolar disorder diagnosis, we are continually faced with many challenges that others don't usually encounter.

Some of these challenges include: job discrimination, unemployment, insomnia, medication (costs and side effects), stigma, alienation, anxiety, and symptom management, to name but a few. While most people experience some of these challenges, it is fair to state that individuals with a mental illness experience most, if not all, of these problems; sometimes all at once.

Consequently, most of us need some form of counseling simply to understand the illness and navigate the difficult obstacles we consistently face throughout our lives.

Seen in this light, counseling isn't a weakness or lack of faith, but a necessity. When mental illness is severe enough, only a few gifted individuals can forgo the counseling process. For the rest of us, it is an extremely important step in the long term recovery process. After a number of years, counseling may become less important, but to minimize its value is unrealistic for most. The illness makes our lives so complicated that it may take years to understand it and develop effective coping skills.

Beyond these reasons for counseling, there are also other persuasive arguments for learning about the mind.

Mental illness profoundly affects our lives as we struggle with unstable thoughts and feelings. This often requires us to bring into our awareness all the areas of the mind that are unknown or avoided. For example, an emotion like anger may actually be experienced as a depressed state of mind; anxiety and fear may descend into a feeling of overall helplessness. Manic thoughts, on the other hand, may be, in part, genuine experiences of creativity and upliftment.

The point is, our thoughts and feelings cannot be ignored. Hidden needs and desires affect behavior in some ways whether we are aware of it or not. This ability to bring these concepts and emotions into our awareness can often be helpful in managing symptoms. This informed point of view is useful for both personal and social growth.

Implied in this wish to understand the mind is the desirability of identifying various thought and emotional patterns existing within us. Simply put, "mind patterns" are habitual ways of [thinking / feeling / acting] that can be largely unconscious. They often affect behavior, creating a kind of knee jerk reaction to the way we view ourselves and handle situations. Two of my own thought patterns that have affected me for many years involve traumatic experiences and catastrophic thinking.

For me, there are two thought / emotional patterns associated with traumatic events I experienced with completely different explanations.

Having briefly been in Cook County jail on 2 occasions, I have an aversion to people touching me on the shoulder from behind. When I'm awakened from sleep, it almost always startles me. Although these incarceration incidents were very difficult, my reaction is understandable. My experience is hardly unique. Cook County Jail is now the second largest mental health care provider in the United States.

Some traumatic experiences are not so insidious, yet surprisingly more enigmatic. For many years I had an occasional feeling of suspense and excitement followed by an intense feeling of alarm. There are certainly any number of agonizing experiences that could account for this feeling of alarm (terror). However, the truth is very surprising.

When I was a boy, our family visited my uncle's resort called Hanson's Hotel. We watched fireworks displays every summer on the

July 4th. Included in these displays were fireworks that instead of dissipating various designs and colors, exploded like an extraordinary clap of thunder. Having discovered the source of this traumatic event, it no longer haunted my memories. Without the help of a counselor, I probably would have never found the source of this anxiety.

Catastrophic thinking is another thought pattern that I unconsciously developed over the years that has caused a lot of extra stress. In this pattern, I automatically interpret a situation in the worst possible way. If I had some minor problem occur in my life, I would assume it would evolve into a major crisis.

For example, if I lost my homework, I imagined I would fail the course I was taking, flunk out of school, become unemployed, and so never be able to afford to live on my own.

Thankfully, by understanding this tendency for catastrophic thinking, I was able to identify the pattern, leading to a more conscious awareness of my thoughts and emotions in various circumstances.

The most difficult thought patterns to overcome are those which evolved over a lifetime.

Sometimes called "conditioning" these systems of thoughts and feelings are usually learned through the constant interaction and repetition of environmental influences. They are like recordings continuously playing in our heads. Often they aren't identified even though they affect our emotions and behavior. This can lead to self-defeating behavior and the loss of relationships.

For example, if someone is conditioned to believe that they aren't worthy of success ("You're a failure and you'll always be a failure!", "You don't deserve i.t") that belief may lead to repeated failures and an overall negative self-concept. In this situation, counseling can be indispensable, if these thoughts are to be identified, understood and overcome.

In addition to revealing thought patterns, counselors can also bring to light some surprising revelations often unnoticed in relationships.

For example, historically, when the family dynamic has been considered, it has mostly been seen from the perspective of the family and their effect on the individual who was ill. But the truth is usually not so easily discerned. The individual suffering from the illness can also affect the family in a substantive way that is equally important and sometimes unanticipated.

This necessary, two-way approach helps reveal the sources of conflict without attempting to assign blame. _Both_ _sides must be understood._ For me, my extreme sensitivity and tendency toward catastrophic thinking caused me to overreact to every situation while others probably would not have reacted so intensely to the same circumstances.

To be sure, psychology offers many helpful approaches for uncovering these tendencies and patterns. Counselors can be a very important resource for an individual searching for self-esteem and personal growth. Counseling can also be an important first step in discovering meaningful states of consciousness.

In my view, it is nearly impossible for most people to explore different forms of consciousness without being aware of their thoughts, emotions, memories and desires. While circumventing the process is certainly possible, it is unrealistic. Deep seated thoughts and feelings can't be ignored without them appearing in other forms.

Precipitating Factors / Triggering Events

The concept of precipitating factors is often overlooked. Precipitating factors are events that initiate or promote the onset of illness, disease, accident, or behavioral response.

These factors can directly influence the way any individual thinks and feels. Some of the most common include: changes in routine, physical illness, divorce, weather changes, a day's history, overall history, a death in the family...

While these factors are very important sources of stress for people, for individuals with a mental illness, they can be even more difficult to bear.

Their actions are sometimes misinterpreted by others. These thoughts and feelings are dismissed, at least in part, as "medication problems". An understanding of these precipitating factors can be very useful in helping individuals cope with their illness.

Another set of factors, are labeled "triggering events". This is a psychological concept that is understood differently by many. Generally, triggering events are defined as incidents that can be identified as the immediate cause for the onset of bipolar disorder or an immediate crisis. Since the illness is generally believed to be a genetic disease that often manifests when some significant event occurs – such as a family death, job loss, divorce, retirement, major change in residence – it is believed the event itself is the catalyst that sets the illness in motion. There are two major limitations to most triggering event explanations.

First, I have known individuals who look back at the triggering event and have interpreted the situation itself as being the point where their future was stolen from them. Consequently, they tend to blame those involved and themselves for their illness.

Second, a more compelling limitation of these triggering event theories concerns the nature of the events in general. What person can go through life without experiencing some major form of stress for any length of time? To be human is to experience countless traumatic events over a lifetime. It is my suspicion that any number of triggering events could cause the illness to manifest. Professionals probably pick the most recent one.

This assertion that some triggering event causes the onset of bipolar disorder tends to give individuals and their families a specific reason for the illness and so provide a kind of closure. In my view, if individuals have a severe predisposition for the disease, they are probably going to experience it regardless. It is extraordinarily difficult, even impossible, to ensure these triggering events don't reoccur during an individual's life.

Projection

There are many factors that influence behavior. For me, the most relevant one has been my reliance on an unproductive coping mechanism called "projection". Various counselors have taught me to recognize this self-defeating behavior in my life. To some extent, I've been able to move beyond it. In essence, projection defines my tendency to blame my problems on others. This defensive behavior was a crutch I used allowing me to dodge responsibility for my actions. Although it is true that I *was* sometimes the victim of ill treatment and discrimination, many more times it was my own attitudes and actions turning me in the wrong direction. With the help of good counselors, I have been able to forgive others and myself for past experiences which kept bubbling up into the present.

Counseling also helped me understand how I projected blame on to others in other circumstances as well. Sometimes stressful situations occurred in which there was actually no one at fault. By seeking to blame others, I was simply being unfair through my misinterpretation of events. Although I still find myself engaging in this unproductive coping mechanism, at least I now recognize it for what it is.

Counselors can also be very helpful in a number of other ways. In addition to helping us to learn about thoughts and feelings, good counselors have the ability to assist us navigate the complicated life experiences we encounter. These situations include financial difficulties, stress management, and relationship problems. All these challenges can require the development of complex strategies that an exceptionally good counselor can help facilitate.

This navigation process goes beyond any one individual's mental health concerns. Virtually every individual struggling with a major mental illness faces the daunting task of figuring out the inner workings of various governmental agencies such as the health care systems and education settings. Without expert assistance, these institutions frustrate and overwhelm. Often individuals don't get the help they need and deserve.

Finally, for many of us struggling with a mental illness, life can be a lonely and sometimes frightening experience. With seemingly few genuine opportunities, life can lack any true sense of purpose. Loneliness and boredom make things even harder because it is sometimes difficult to find ways to challenge our intelligence while also minimizing stress. Counselors can often help identify these situations and suggest coping skills and other strategies that can make life better. This, in turn, can lead to empowerment and even long term recovery.

Many of the opportunities and assistance I have received have been the result of wonderful counselors who have helped me find the resources I needed.

7. Creativity: A Malady and a Remedy

This chapter explores some aspects of mental illness that are clearly discernable as forms of creative expression. Because the symptoms of bipolar disorder can be so difficult to identify and manage, these creative impulses are usually misinterpreted as evidence of the illness or discounted entirely.

Once again, I need to be absolutely clear. When I was mentally ill, I had a lot of uncontrolled and misdirected energy that took the form of mania, depression, and delusions. The crises were so dangerous they sometimes were life threatening. It was bewildering to my parents and mental health professionals who were trying to help me. I, myself, was unable to verbalize what was happening to me. It was only years later that I began to understand my illness and its creative potential.

In actuality, there are, indeed, some creative aspects of bipolar disorder and its treatment manifesting during an individual's psychotic episodes that can be useful and even therapeutic in the difficult process of long term recovery. Beyond the almost stereotypical notion that assumes creativity merely helps people with mental illness express their feelings, creativity can also be seen as an essential process for individuals who need to tap into their artistic intelligence. By identifying, controlling, and directing this creative impulse, individuals with bipolar disorder may be able to better cope with symptoms and manage stress. Most forms of creative endeavor can improve self-esteem and self-confidence, as they provide individuals opportunities to redefine their identity in positive ways.

[See Chapter:*10 Valuable Coping Strategies*, Strategy 10 – Creativity]

This creativity is a major reason for our inner journey. While life is a journey for everyone, individuals with a mental illness travel through life in rather unique and indecipherable ways. This sojourn of self-discovery can be very painful and lonely. This whole process is so subjective and society's attitudes so "scientific," that creativity is primarily seen as symptoms of the illness. This illness usually returns periodically throughout most of our lives; so we must be aware of our creative intelligence, beliefs, and life styles because they are usually essential for long term recovery.

The creative process may be expressed through art - writing in my case. This creativity documents states of mind and interprets the artist's experience. This process of self-discovery helps in testing ideas and beliefs and assists the individual in understanding their life.

The journey often involves discovering new interests in books and philosophies considered foreign to our culture. For example, some religious seekers assert the notion that we are all God. In the West, it is fair to say that this idea is considered wrong and even blasphemous. But for individuals with a mental illness, it provides a different way of understanding the world.

I'm not suggesting that delusional thoughts during a psychotic break are safe or even desirable; however, these unconventional ideas do strongly infer that western science and traditional religious concepts are sometimes ill equipped to address the kind of creative expression they may encounter when interacting with the mentally ill.

Another way to explain the relationship between creativity and mental illness is to explore the well metaphor that "life is a stage" as Shakespeare once wrote. The great playwright and countless others have portrayed life as a kind a cosmic drama in which we all play various roles. As life goes on, we play a number of different roles, sometimes simultaneously. Then we eventually leave the stage and take our experiences with us.

"All the world's a stage, and all the men and women merely players. They have their exits and their entrances; and one person in their time plays many parts..."

THE PROMISE OF LONG TERM RECOVERY

Shakespeare from the play "As You Like It" Act 2, Scene 7

This metaphor is useful in describing individuals with bipolar disorder. Many of us create our own stories when we are ill that are disconnected from the more objective reality of daily life. We become the main character in a personal narrative. We use original plot lines, rituals, and props to help us find our way through the various chapters of "our book". These stories can be so convincing that others sometimes unwittingly join in the plot without discerning that the mental illness is present. However, since almost everyone else doesn't recognize these extremely subjective aspects of our thoughts and behavior, we are seen as psychotic only and potentially dangerous.

Certainly, to a large extent, individuals in this state are clearly ill and in need of treatment. Someone trapped in their own story can have tortured obsessive thoughts and may even engage in risky behavior. These obsessive thoughts can feel as if the individuals are standing in front of a locked door while the walls are closing in. Frantically, searching through countless keys, they attempt to discover the one to escape. Even more disturbing are the many perilous behaviors we may engage in when we are uninhibited. Reckless driving and directing traffic were two very dangerous behaviors I engaged in.

Even after individuals recover, this deep seated creative yearning will most likely return. Even when coping skills such as medication, meditation, and exercise are utilized, this primal need may still endure. Like an invisible wave incessantly seeking some shore, this creative energy never rests for long. If it is not identified and developed, it may repeatedly flood the mind, uninvited. Then, the entire cycle begins once again, and relapse may be harder to elude.

Since creativity is subjective, I will discuss it in terms of my own experience. For me, writing is a way to redirect mania and delusional thinking; so I don't continually "slide over the edge" into psychotic states, turning my life upside down. By writing poems and stories, I am able to carefully control and channel my creative energy without becoming overwhelmed by it. Many forms of literature and art contain some redirected delusional thinking in one form or another. An author writing a war epic, for example, needs to imagine all kinds of dangerous people, places, and events. Isn't writing - and art in general - a way to redirect and channel all kinds of thought and emotional patterns? Actors have to "make themselves" into another person to fulfill a role. [See Chapter: *Famous People with Bipolar Disorder*]

When it comes to mental illness, creativity is usually addressed only in passing, if at all. This can inhibit an individual's chances for genuine self-expression and long term recovery. This creative expression is a fundamental yearning for most of us with a mental illness. It doesn't go away by ignoring it. Imaginative writing and other forms of art are often legitimate ways to express these creative thoughts before they become problematic. Delusional thoughts and actions do manifest because of the illness, but creative projects may be useful in redirecting these symptoms in positive ways before they threaten to become a problem.

In addition to thoughts, one of the biggest challenges many of us face is the problem of managing emotions. Often we are like paper towels empathically soaking up every feeling we encounter. We feel too deeply and intensely making us vulnerable in almost every situation.

Many of us have a passion for life that constantly leaves us expecting more. Our incessant need for rapid change and our desire for excitement often lead to unrealistic expectations and disappointment. This is greatly magnified when the illness surfaces and overwhelms our thoughts and feelings. These tendencies can lead to self-absorption which may lead to extreme introversion and depression.

However, when creativity is available in some form of art, these thoughts and feelings are better understood, leading to a more comprehensive strategy for managing symptoms. For example, one of the most important aspects of any artist's creative life is to make sense of existence. It is only through self-knowledge that an artist can really come to understand their own mind and the surrounding world. Self-inquiry and counseling can help explain these inner and outer realms in detail, giving access to them in a variety of artistic ways. This can help create a sense of closure concerning the past and allow for a new understanding that expands consciousness as the present unfolds.

This self-expression is another reason why the "lived experience" is so powerful in creative art. The unique and highly unusual lives we are living allow for more comprehensive notions about life and what it means to be human. When these perceptions and experiences are recorded, after a time of inner reflection, creativity can become a strategy taking us beyond our limitations and fears.

One of the most important character traits to develop for creative expression is self-discipline. Many courageous attitudes are often required including the willingness to face the truth about our illness and the ability to accept new ideas. As both witness and participant, we must be constantly vigilant in the process of synthesizing our thoughts and feelings, as new situations arise. We must take these unique experiences lending themselves to artistic expression, and allow them to blossom into new ideas and progressive insights, valuable to the reader/ viewer and ourselves. This attitude often requires an extraordinary amount of imagination and self-discipline; but it is very helpful for developing strategies that enhance long term recovery. In time, insights about ourselves and the world can be integrated into our daily lives, helping us remain healthy and creative.

More practically, self-discipline takes the form of following strict routines as well as creating and maintaining valuable coping skills.

In this way, artistic expression can become a "way of being" and other areas of life can evolve around it. In order to write a novel, for instance, a writer must live in two worlds at the same time. To use the imagination freely, the other areas of life may need to be as predictable as possible. For me, chores like mowing the lawn and cleaning the house become ways to "ground" myself with physical work, so my thoughts are more disciplined and less scattered.

[See Chapter: *10 Valuable Coping Strategies*, Strategies 1, 3]

Habits I try to maintain – such as resisting the temptation to drink alcohol – help insure a manic episode isn't triggered or a depression doesn't descend. Probably most important of all, I always try to get enough sleep. Without it, symptoms begin to appear, and I become miserable with little creative energy available.

[See Chapter:*10 Valuable Coping Strategies*, Strategy 4]

By creating these safety nets, I was gradually able to improve my writing and create a genuine sense of purpose that my jobs and relationships often couldn't provide. Ironically, the predictability of my environment allowed me to pursue my imaginative thoughts to a much greater degree than I ever thought possible.

Life is not so easily controlled. The impermanence and mutability of events and situations usually overwhelm attempts to create order in some rigid fashion. However, by regulating life as much as possible and limiting the number of distractions around me, a more productive inner space has slowly unfolded. Using writing as a coping skill in a variety of circumstances has helped me to improve many otherwise troubling situations. [See Chapter:*10 Valuable Coping Strategies*, Strategies 3, 4, 10]

In particular, coping skills have been very effective in shaping and directing thoughts and feelings. Jogging and meditation, for example, consistently sort, manage, and control my mind, so that my writing can be pursued on a regular basis. Often, the writing itself successfully redirects my thoughts and emotions and steers me away from frustration and alienation. Because my mind still remains restless and unpredictable at times, these skills help me to remain busy as well.

[See Chapter:*10 Valuable Coping Strategies*, Strategies 1, 2]

For individuals with bipolar disorder, our minds can be our best friends or our worst enemies. Engaged in meaningful productive activities, we can excel in any number of endeavors. When left to its own devices, the mind can manufacture many kinds of doubts, fears, and anxieties. Self-discipline is vital for both creative expression and daily living.

The whole creative process can be exceptionally useful since it addresses so many elements of mental health. It can help manage a number of problematic tendencies such as the constant desire for change, the incessant need for excitement, and the underlying need to create. For me, writing is a way to engage these tendencies in a disciplined manner thereby managing their influence.

One of the most difficult things to manage is coping with boredom in its many forms. Due to our challenges, both personal and social, we are often denied access to interesting and engaging employment opportunities. Creative expression can be a real source of fulfillment even while working tedious and unrewarding jobs. I believe creativity can help combat boredom and dissatisfaction by redirecting their impact, before they can trigger a manic or depressive episode.

Boredom and loneliness can be so unbearable that individuals sometimes "drift off" into mania and depression just to escape their misery. These emotions can be contributing factors for relapse. One reason my own delusions were so intense was that my life was empty of genuine meaning. "Coming down" from the psychosis was so painful for me was because I was "forced" back into an extremely limiting life with no authentic opportunities.

There are three specific ideas about creative writing that are unique to my own process, but may also be useful to others.

1. I write on unlined paper. Lined paper has inherent boundaries and structure. It also reminds me of the academic baggage of my highly regimented school years.

2. I never ask for opinions about my work. For most of us with a mental illness, we have been told what to think and how to feel and act for so long, it seems nothing original is left within us. Instead of soliciting feedback, I ask my wife, Donna, to read my work; and she makes only supportive comments. This may sound self-serving; however, my writing has greatly improved over the years. I don't write with the feeling that others are looking over my shoulder.

3. My attitude. I always try to remember that the ability to write is a precious gift that to be used to express truth and beauty as best as I can. This attitude helps me write honestly and with sincerity.

8. 10 Reasons Creativity is so Important to Develop

For some of us with a serious mental illness creativity can be a powerful way to redirect our thoughts, feelings, and energy that is both therapeutic and fulfilling. Together with medication, physical exercise, and daily meditation, creativity is indispensable for many of us who are challenged with a bipolar diagnosis. (The strategy numbers are from the Chapter *10 Valuable Coping Strategies*)

1. Clarifies Thoughts

Creativity can help redirect delusional impulses. We can express ourselves in socially acceptable ways. Writing, painting, and singing may help channel this energy before it overwhelms. Ignoring or burying this creative propensity doesn't insure it won't return. Delusional thoughts may contribute to a possible relapse if left unguarded. The idea is to manage the impact. <u>Strategy 10</u>

2. Increases Self-Knowledge

We're usually required to undergo extensive counseling. We must learn about our thought and emotional patterns, repressed feelings, and conditioning experiences. We need to understand how we interact with the world generally. This can be an unanticipated bonus of the counseling process. Strategy 9

3. Enhances Concentration

Creativity is a different form of concentration, somewhat disconnected from normal states of mind. A predictable routine and physical work can help balance the creative aspects of thought with the more practical ways of thinking. Strategies 1, 2, 3

4. Lowers Stress And Enhances Self-Confidence

We can't handle a lot of stress because anxiety is often part of the diagnosis. Creative activities are often practiced with no one else around. Working alone, we can fully engage our intelligence without outside pressure. The only stress we may experience is pressure we put on ourselves. Creativity gives us a chance to build self-confidence, maintain a genuine sense of purpose, and overcome boredom.

5. Personal Discovery

We have been analyzed, counseled, and behavior modified to the point we sometimes feel we don't have personal thoughts and feelings. Creativity helps us move beyond theories and labels, so we can discover who we really are. Scientific studies of psychology and the mind are not the final word on consciousness. <u>Strategy 9</u>

6. Resolves The Effects Of Difficult Experiences

For me, creativity provides a sense of closure , helping resolve festering emotions and unresolved conflict. I think about a problem, such as a memory like Cook County jail, and I write about it. I often experience a cathartic feeling of moving past the experience. Sometimes I can capture the actual feeling, describe it, and then let it go. Painting, singing, and dancing may also be effective. Creativity keeps my mind positively occupied, so it doesn't have the chance to manufacture doubt, anxiety, and restlessness. <u>Strategy 6</u>

7. Openness To New Experiences And Possibilities

Creativity gives the openness for experiencing unforeseen possibilities. Before my illness, I was close-minded, ridiculing ideas and practices I didn't understand. I once believed medication and meditation were both worthless until I desperately needed them to live a productive life. <u>Strategies 2, 7</u>

8. Generating Original Ideas

We don't _think_ outside the box, we _live_ outside the box. To survive, we have adapted to our situation. It's a steep learning curve, giving us unique viewpoints and insights. When ill, we may think we're a religious figure; when well, we might see a statue trapped in granite. When ill, we may speak unintelligibly; when well, we can be very perceptive. For many, reality is often experimental, so often we generate original ideas. <u>Strategies 9, 10</u>

9. Exploring Other World Views

In our relentless search for relief, we discover books, places, and individuals we never would have sought out, enhancing our creative pursuits. For example, by learning about Eastern philosophy, I was able to understand the concept of time as a circle rather than a straight line. This helped me to think and write from a different perspective.

10. Expanded Awareness

Creativity expands awareness. In the creative process we grow spiritually by developing self-discipline. Upon finishing a creation, we become a different, more mature person. Thoughts that once led to mental illness like "wrong turns" and "crash landings" no longer influence us. We have evolved to a new expanded level of understanding.

9. Spirituality and Evolution

I have left this chapter on spirituality for last as it is best understood within the context of medication, psychology, and creativity. It is necessary to stress the importance of these ideas as a prerequisite to any sustainable search for the Divine.

There is an adage: "leap and the net will appear". (*John Burroughs*) However, for many of us with bipolar disorder, "leap and the police will appear" is also true. As the ending chapter it insures that the need for balance and long term recovery are emphasized first.

Beginning the Journey

Some of my ideas about God and spirituality come from direct experience; others originated in books written by mystics I have come to trust. These ideas have helped me gain some insight into the human condition especially as it relates to my own mental illness.

One of the universal principles frequently associated with spirituality is the notion that life is a kind of quest or perpetual journey, never allowing us to stop and rest for long. Constantly in motion and ruled by change, we are driven by an inner force or energy incessantly guiding us forward. The stages of birth, growth, decline, and death require us to adapt both internally and externally; the quest for certainty, permanence, and love never ceases. On this journey, many of us with bipolar disorder are required to evolve quickly to discover ways to recover and stay well. This driving force of energy, sometimes called consciousness, is difficult, if not impossible to control. Life can feel overwhelming with no reliable trail markers to help us find our way.

This conscious energy can sometimes lead us into psychosis; if left uncontrolled becomes ever more challenging due to the chemical imbalances we are required to confront., Medications are then frequently portrayed as undesirable because they somehow block this energy to the point that it closes off creative inspiration and spiritual experience. Conversely, some describe bipolar disorder as a *only* a disease with no genuine spiritual value.

It has often been asserted that "*God* is infinite" and "*God* can do anything". Since God is infinite, doesn't it follow that there are many, many ways to reach that Divine? Couldn't medications to address bipolar disorder also be a part of our quest? When our conscious energy is so powerful, yet unstable, it seems to me that channeling it renders it much more beneficial in every kind of endeavor.

Even with the medication, this energy is sometimes diverted into an avalanche of unruly thoughts and emotions that are difficult to manage. The lows of deep depression and the anguish of mania can feel like the world has left us behind and we don't belong here.

Ironically, these very same emotions can also be sources of rapid growth and spiritual maturity. The illness nearly always requires us to change our attitudes and behavior, our entire lives are affected. The old and familiar ways of living become detrimental to our health and usually feel worn out and hollow.

The experiences of fear and alienation that accompany these changes are very painful. Yet buried within these challenges are the seeds of spiritual evolution. Over time, in order to survive, the old ways of perceiving the world are abandoned. We are required to change and reinvent ourselves. This can create a more expansive awareness; a new and more spiritual individual emerges who apprehends the world with a more subtle and valuable way of being.

Spiritual values gradually supersede the psychological concepts of conditioning and self-destructive. This transformation can occur within anyone, but individuals with bipolar disorder are often required to change drastically and continually simply to survive and recover.

Modern science consistently refuses to acknowledge this spiritual transformation process, insisting on observing and interpreting only the external world. This bias accepts the body and mind with no recognition of the spirit. In this approach, the kingdom of God is "without" not "within". It explains away or ignores anything that cannot be measured, counted, or dissected. Since many basic scientific theories are found to be obsolete after a few years, science sees truth as relative - changing as science "progresses".

Scientific knowledge and technology has provided countless lifesaving breakthroughs in every field, including medicine. Yet, it has also created every kind of destructive weapon and has produced a craze of waste. The application of scientific knowledge in technology often proceeds regardless of the consequences.

This fixation with the outer world has led to the rejection of serious exploration of the inner world. Like a man who has lost his watch in the forest, and searches for it under a street lamp because there is more light, material science denies the spiritual world because it is looking in the wrong place. This predilection reaches the level of absurdity when we consider the Russian cosmonaut who was orbiting the earth and triumphantly reported that he could find no evidence of God around him. It is difficult to understand how people with multiple "PhDs" still have no real understanding of spiritual principles.

Nevertheless, the inner world of the spirit exists. Hidden within the body-mind complex, spirit is the vast ocean of existence within all and yet transcending it. The body, generally speaking, is the vessel for the mind. It is born, grows, declines, dies and returns to the elements. It is a vehicle in which we travel on our journey. The mind, on the other hand, is a vast network of thoughts and feelings through which we perceive and experience the world. In the mind are all the latent and conscious tendencies, both noble and contemptible. The mind has convinced itself that it is the ultimate reality, and consequently assumes that there is nothing else to seek beyond it. This is sometimes called the "ego" or "lower self".

Beyond the realm of the ego exists the world of Spirit. Its existence is real, but it is so clouded over by the senses and desires that it is not recognized as the transcendental Divine Energy within everything. The mind is simply a vast collection of thoughts, feelings, and tendencies creating the illusion of permanence; created in part by memory. Our dependence on thought is like caterpillars going from leaf to leaf – we rarely depart from one until we grasp another. If we do somehow find ourselves between thoughts, we immediately sense that there is only "nothingness". This revelation can be so frightening that we immediately grasp at the "leaf or strand" of thought again. This keeps the mind intact and in charge.

This "nothingness" hidden within the mind is something. It is in the space between thoughts. It is <u>this</u> moment that always truly exists, unencumbered by the ego's interference. This awareness of a more expanded form of consciousness, if explored, gradually opens for longer periods, so that an apprehension of the present moment is possible.

The past is gone and kept alive only through memories. The future doesn't exist; it is a set of expectations that are projections of desires and tendencies. This experience of the moment is not limited; it doesn't divide time into fragments.

This allows the spirit to become ever more discernable. When the mind is still, and thoughts and feelings gradually dissolve, the "kingdom within" begins to take hold in the form of intuitive consciousness.

It can be a very difficult task to overcome the mind, even temporarily, because it incessantly seeks to satisfy its own wants and needs like recognition and self-satisfaction. The tendency of the mind is to increase these desires which, in turn, create new ones. These expectations are never fully realized, and dissatisfaction may lead to frustration and anger. The mind is so overwhelmed by its own priorities that life itself can become an unending cycle of anticipation and disappointment.

Even when most of us – and I include myself here – claim to have surrendered to God, in actuality we just shift the focus of our minds' tendencies to more subtle desires such as the wish to "advance spiritually" or the desire to become "more spiritual" than others (spiritual elitism). Our never ending striving for recognition and achievement is redirected to our community, service projects and our relationships.

Ironically, those of us living with a mental illness may be less affected by such "spiritual" drives because we are often unsuccessful in filling leadership roles in any kind of organization. This gives us the potential to walk the path of spiritual discovery without the temptation of forging ahead in selfishness. We can live in the moment at times and experience pure consciousness. This can help transform alienation and boredom into opportunities to experience inner silence and peace.

Science generally has no interest in this spiritual awakening process. It doesn't recognize the crucial relationship between mental illness and spirituality. Due to this lack of understanding, science is unable to perceive that mental illnesses themselves, like bipolar disorder, are in part motivated by the Divine Energy that is fused to the mind. This energy pushes the mind ever onward testing the limits of the ego's domain. Since very few can circumvent this process, most individuals with a mental illness are required to pass through and go beyond these difficult states. Since "psychotic episodes" are both dangerous and alluring, they represent a challenge to evolve beyond.

In addition to this divine impulse, there are other reasons why individuals with bipolar disorder are sometimes misunderstood when they turn to spirituality. Often, we have nothing to lose because relationships can be fleeting, and opportunities are extremely limited. With no genuine purpose to sustain us, loneliness, boredom, and stigma challenge our self-confidence and rob us of our dignity. With no other resources to sustain us, we go within for reassurance and acceptance.

Sometimes individuals even willfully become ill simply to escape a reality that is so harsh that anything else seems better. In a delusional state of mind, for example, individuals will create their own spiritual stories superimposed upon the external world casting themselves as important religious characters. I believe, these states of mind have a slight degree of spiritual authenticity to them; making it difficult to determine where the psychosis ends and spirituality begins. This blurring of mental illness and spirituality can be even more difficult to understand when a genuine spiritual experience is later mentally exaggerated prompting delusional behavior in its wake.

Rituals

Rituals are a useful example to explain the way in which individuals with bipolar disorder engage in spiritual activities when they are ill. This behavior is usually defined by mental health professionals as "meaningless, repetitive actions over an extended period of time". These rituals are seen to be repeated because obsessive thoughts are leading to compulsive actions. They are usually identified as symptoms of an illness - a kind of religiosity seeking to avoid problems by fixating on religion.

These medical diagnoses are simplistic at best. Rituals have been part of social, personal and religious activities for thousands of years. For example, in the Roman Catholic faith, the "mass" is a complex ritual, others are the sign of the cross, and the prayer of the rosary. In Hinduism, the temple puja (ceremonial worship), mala beads (prayer beads), and arati (a part of puja using flames) are clearly forms of ritual. In Tibetan Buddhism, death rites, and mantras can also be associated with rituals as well. In fact, throughout history, rituals have been and continue to be a vital part or organized religion.

Personal rituals, may include bathing, tooth brushing, grooming and dressing, eating meals, laundry, shopping usually done at a specific time and order

Social rituals may be sponsored by the government – like putting flags on veterans' graves on Memorial Day, fireworks on July 4th, lighting the national Christmas tree in Washington, D.C. Marriage is often a combination of a social and religious ritual. Even traffic laws may be seen as kind of ritual – waiting for traffic light colors, merging into traffic and yielding to pedestrians.

So, how do some of these obsessive rituals performed by the mentally ill compare with the codified rituals of religion? As I understand it, obsessive thoughts, which are unwanted and unrelenting, are eased by the performance of compulsive actions. These actions relieve the mind from the unwanted thoughts when they occur. In essence, the compulsive actions are ways for the mind to "let go" of the obsessive thinking patterns for a while. For example, if someone is always afraid that an intruder could enter their room, they may repeatedly lock their door. They may also lock their door a specific number of times because that number is considered to be a lucky one. The intended result is to relieve the anxiety associated with the thoughts occurring in various situations.

These obsessive rituals associated with mental illness can be closely identified with religious practices. Both types of ritual (psychotic and religious) can be performed to obtain a specific result, such as securing God's grace. The rituals' purposes may be to receive help, achieve success, or insure a closer connection to the Divine.

In my case, this wish for a closer relationship to God became tangled up in my delusional thinking because of a manic episode. I was not prepared for the experience itself when it happened. As a result, deep seated desires for recognition and wealth were magnified and became more dangerous because of my mental illness. In one instance, I tossed all of my possessions into a dumpster in the middle of the night while cleaning my apartment of every speck of dirt, so God would be pleased and answer my prayer for fame.

Not surprisingly, while I was a resident in state mental health facilities, I sometimes heard about or actually witnessed other residents seeking God's help. One man I encountered described an altar he had built in his room that seemed to be very similar to the altar used by Roman Catholics. He believed he was communicating with God in this way. Another behavior I witnessed repeatedly involved the residents touching the TV screen whenever a minister promised salvation. In their desperation, these individuals performed the behavior hoping for relief.

There are two important ideas here.

First, almost all ritualistic behavior is probably purposeful to some degree. Sometimes it can reflect an effort to find relief and discover a genuine sense of purpose.

Second, this search can include the longing for God, an explanation for behavior, even if shrouded deep in an individual's mental illness.

Simply dismissing these rituals as symptoms is somewhat limiting. But, there are strange similarities about the rituals performed by the mentally ill that are not easily explained away as symptoms.

Common behaviors associated with the use of numbers, newspapers, and the obsession with certain beliefs, create the feeling that the behaviors may have differing story lines but similar props and themes. This suggests these rituals are buried deep within our collective unconscious and were once important. Maybe our distant ancestors used these unorthodox behaviors to enhance their skills, explain their world, and transcend their mortality. I don't believe these rituals performed in the context of mental illness are harmless or even desirable; however, they do suggest there is some common source behind them, beyond what the symptoms might suggest.

There are certainly many problems with these rituals that are difficult to ignore. They often have the force and power of a religious experience. They are difficult to interrupt, even when dangerous situations develop. Sometimes individuals become very angry when they are thwarted from obtaining objects they believe are needed to perform these rituals. This rage can be difficult to understand because these activities usually make no sense to family, friends, and law enforcement.

But there are still other less insidious reasons why rituals are troublesome. For thousands of years there have been wide open areas in which rituals could be performed without obstacles like highways, skyscrapers, and fences. For the vast majority of us, the days of following any trails created by ritualistic maps has long since passed. We can no longer follow natural tracks or signs in order to seek answers. So, any attempt to embrace these rites is usually frustrating and potentially dangerous.

For those of us with a mental illness, very difficult challenges concerning rituals is their subjectivity. We often stubbornly cling to our own distorted understanding of events even years later. More specifically, we often observe two things happening at the same time and assume we caused the event.

For example, I was singing Don McLean's song "Starry, Starry, Night" for hours as I was walking around a university campus. At one point, the lyrics contained the word "snow" in them. It started to snow at the same time. (It was April). I assumed that I had caused it to snow.

Another embarrassing example involved a freight train. When the train was passing, I walked right behind the last car. I interpreted this behavior to mean that I was "on the right track" and that my rituals were directing my story. In actuality, I had simply adjusted my stride to coincide with the train, but I assumed that I had magically controlled its speed.

Over the years, there were a number of these situations that I misinterpreted and often involving TV shows and music. These rituals often evolved into "secret missions" that were all-consuming at times.

Rituals themselves still represent attempts to understand spiritual concepts by relying on the external world. As I mentioned earlier, it is modern science's dependence on observations based on the outer world that has limited its effectiveness in attempts to search for the divine. In my view, a similar problem exists with the rituals I engaged in during my episodes of mental illness. For me, and I suspect for others, the external world is constantly shifting and any kind of permanence is difficult to find. Rituals may provide different and unique perspectives of the world, but they still rely on the outer world to be the important place to search for truth.

For me, even though these unusual practices were very beneficial in expressing creative thoughts and emotions, they were not helpful in discovering and exploring the world of the spirit. I needed the stability of medication and counseling. The medication was eventually effective in managing the symptoms of my illness, such as delusional thinking, deep depression, and manic states of mind. Counseling was equally important in understanding thought patterns, resolving problems, and directing creative impulses. These strategies of both medication and counseling provided the foundation on which I *could* develop spiritually.

Meditation

Strange as it may sound, even with medication and counseling, anxiety and restlessness were still major problems. It was only after reading the book *Journey of Awakening,* by Ram Dass, a former Harvard professor, that I was finally able to cobble together an exceedingly helpful meditative technique. It allowed me to "get inside my own head" and begin to examine how fast my thoughts were moving, so I could sort out the kinds of thoughts I was thinking. The meditation process allowed me to witness my anxious thoughts, leading to a better understanding of their meaning. It helped identify my tendency to dwell on the past which led to thoughts of despair. By practicing meditation for only twenty minutes a day, I was able to continue my education and pursue a career.

Without meditation, I would have probably returned to expressing my need for spiritual experience by falling back into ritualistic thought patterns and behavior. With no other strategy available to help me find my way, I might very well have relied again on the symptoms of bipolar disorder as a way to find the answers I sought. This would have probably led to more institutions and less personal freedom.

There were also other unexpected benefits to meditation. By helping control my restless thoughts and gradually dissolving impulsive tendencies, my sense of despair lifted. I found that I could write with more precision and originality. Instead of writing stories and poems that were so subjective they were almost nonsensical, meditation allowed me to integrate psychological and creative thoughts more harmoniously. Consequently, these writings were also understandable to others. Over time, my stories and poems improved because they were coherent while still imaginative.

Emotional maturity and spiritual development were among the most significant and surprising benefits of daily meditation. These qualities gradually eclipsed most other desires as the search for spiritual fulfillment was enhanced by emotional strength and moral growth. Because of meditation, I now don't fall into the old delusional states in an attempt to find God in the external world. In addition, meditation has brought me a sense of strength which allows me to experience relief from my illness.

So, meditation has become one of the most important coping skills in my "tool box". Like so many other things, I was skeptical and arrogant about it whenever it was mentioned on TV or in conversation. I only turned to it in utter desperation. Without it I most certainly would not have been able to live a normal life, because medication and counseling alone did not allow me to sustain a long term recovery. Meditation, which has been beneficial for both my mental health and spiritual discovery, has also forged a measure of emotional stability and self-reliance, areas on which I still continually work.

Developing Self-Awareness

In addition to meditation, there are other ways in which mental illness can serve as a catalyst for spiritual growth. Many times, the thoughts and feelings associated with mental illness are unbearable. This sense of agony, fear, and despair often requires us to adapt quickly. After a while, the recognition of wrong turns and "crash landings" serve to point out which directions to avoid. As this painful process continues, old thought patterns are discarded and, often in desperation, some of us move beyond traditional concepts of religion.

Because of stigma and societal prejudice, individuals with bipolar disorder often initially seek out spirituality because they have fewer relationships and are exceedingly disappointed with life. We are treated with disrespect and our sense of dignity and self-worth are always at risk.

With no help or support, God alone becomes our source of comfort, and gradually all the disappointments that were once so painful eventually become chances to go within, and so the outer world is no longer the only important way of experiencing life.

Over time, I began to see how my own negative tendencies either created or added to my difficulties. With emotional maturity and spiritual growth, I began to apprehend that everyone's life is difficult and that anger, resentment, and impatience were as much a part of my predicament as was societal indifference. By gradually accepting responsibility for my own problems as they related to others, some of my disappointment disappeared.

This self-awareness that is so painful to acquire is usually the result of being "conscious of consciousness". In other words, because of our mental illness, unique life experiences, and extensive counseling, we become more aware of how our thoughts and feelings affect us and those around us. Even deeply buried thoughts like repressed anger manifesting as depression are seen for what they are. With an understanding of these thought patterns and emotional challenges, the foundations of spirituality are built which slowly redirect self-defeating behaviors and attitudes that are no longer relevant.

Compassion, Forgiveness

Without a doubt, all individuals go through these growth spurts in times of pain and sorrow. It is also true that nobody's life is easy, as I have stressed earlier. But, living with a bipolar disorder is almost never easy for long. Throughout most of our lives, in the relentless search for relief, we are constantly required to experiment, change, and adapt. Our constant need to adjust makes it difficult for others to establish a frame of reference with us, and so they can't truly understand. Thus, spirituality can often fill the void.

There are other spiritual aspects of bipolar disorder that are sometimes ignored or misunderstood as well. For instance, suffering may be the only way to learn true compassion for others. Since it is difficult to teach, yet important to learn, helping others who are also struggling can be very therapeutic and enhance spiritual growth.

Along with compassion, patience and humility are also difficult to acquire. For most of us with a mental illness; our time in schools, hospitals, and other institutions have created a lot of pent up emotions like anger, resentment, and the desire for justice. For me, these thoughts were beginning to poison my mind and infect all aspects of my life. Counseling, however, helped me identify these thoughts and events, so I could consciously give up my attachment to them, forgiving and forgetting as best I could. This helped me to become less fixated on the past. I also learned to be strong enough to recognize my own faults and weaknesses and accept responsibility for them.

Equally important, I was able to forgive myself and learn from my own mistakes, so I could continue to grow spiritually. My issue had always been the failure to take medications. This mistake I made repeatedly until I realized that my life was much, much better when I took them. Taking medications has always required a sense of humility and surrender that is still difficult for me to bear especially around people who are uneducated about mental illness, but these very spiritual qualities often generalize into other situations where humility and the attitude of surrender are also very helpful.

Once my coping skills of meditation, physical exercise, and creative writing began to take hold; my medications were greatly supportive, and I was able to progress more rapidly. What was once a curse has now become a genuine opportunity to expand beyond the boundaries and limitations of my illness. Although my life was once extremely painful and challenging, I now begin to interpret it in retrospect and notice that others around me were all struggling too.

In a sense, for me, suffering has become a kind grace because it requires me to trust in God no matter the circumstances. It requires me to consistently surrender my competitiveness, ambition, and desire for recognition. It has been, and continues to be, a slow process; but it brings me into the present moment more often.

There are things spirituality <u>can't</u> do for me. Most importantly, *it doesn't eliminate the illness itself.* This was one wrong turn I took repeatedly. The physical body, brain, and nervous system are not discounted because of my own pride or an ignorant person's well-meaning advice. Another important point - the need for genuine coping skills that inevitably involve lifestyle changes. Being the designated driver watching everyone else get drunk was far too tempting for me. In addition, health rules can be even more important for individuals with a mental illness. A specific routine that involves sleep, diet, and genuinely meaningful activities are needed for most of us in order to sustain a long term recovery. All these ideas are also useful because they promote a relatively stable environment from which creative and spiritual pursuits can flourish. [See Chapters: *Coping Strategies*, and *10 Valuable Strategies*]

It is the balance between the mundane and the spiritual that has been vital for my health and peace of mind. This stability offers a real sense of purpose, motivating and directing the course of my daily routine. There is an old saying that I heard a while ago that makes sense to me.

> Even as we are searching for God,
> God is searching for us.

In essence, I believe, our deepest yearning is to be with God, and in one way or another that is the purpose and motivation for our existence.

10. A Simple Meditation to Relax the Mind and Body

This practice relaxes the body, slows down the flow of thoughts and emotions, and trains the attention to stay alert and steady.

Position
Close your eyes
Sit on a chair, or the floor
Don't lie down
Back straight, not rigid or arched
In a chair:
> feet flat on the floor
> don't cross the legs or ankles
Hands resting in lap or on thighs
Palms up or down
Fingers relaxed and open

Breathing and Counting
Breathe normally, feeling the breath passing through the nose to the lungs; count each inhale and exhale.

Inhale silently count 1
Exhale silently count 1
Inhale silently count 2
Exhale silently count 2
Continue counting each breath to 10. When reaching 10, return to 1 and start over.

THE PROMISE OF LONG TERM RECOVERY

<u>For these common experiences</u>

Counting past 10
Forgetting the number
Falling asleep

just start over at 1

.

There is no success, no failure
There is no right, no wrong,
Just breathing and counting

11. Famous People with Bipolar Disorder

This Chapter contains a sampling of famous people with bipolar disorder, anxiety, and depression in various walks of life: Actors, Athletes, Authors. Business, Composers, Leaders, Musicians, Painters, Scientists, Television

Actors
Ben Stiller
Carrie Fisher
Catherine Zeta-Jones
Frank Sinatra
Jean Claude Van Damme
Linda Hamilton
Patty Duke
Richard Dreyfuss

JOHN FREDERICK ZURN

Athletes

Daryl Strawberry , baseball
A.J. Mendez (AJ Lee)[1], wrestling
Dwayne ("The Rock") Johnson[2], wrestling
Charles Haley[3], football
Terry Bradshaw[4], football
David Feherty[5], golf
Clint Malarchuk[6], hockey
Justin Peck[7], motorcycle racer
Dorothy Hamill[8], skater
Amanda Beard[9], swimmer
Michael Phelps[10], swimmer

Authors

Charles Dickens
Cynthia M. Sabotka
Edgar Allan Poe
Ernest Hemingway
Herman Hesse
John Keats
Mark Twain
Ralph Waldo Emerson

1.   https://www.bphope.com/aj-mendez-brooks-wrestling-stigma-bipolar/

2.   https://www.hopetocope.com/hope-buzz/dwayne-johnson-opens-up-about-his-depression/

3.   https://www.pro-football-reference.com/players/H/HaleCh00.htm

4.   https://en.wikipedia.org/wiki/Terry_Bradshaw

5.   https://www.bphope.com/david-feherty-bipolar-golf-humor/

6.   https://www.hopetocope.com/men-depression-nhl-goalie-clint-malarchuck/

7.   https://www.bphope.com/justin-peck-living-full-throttle/

8.   https://www.biography.com/athlete/dorothy-hamill

9.   https://amandabeardofficial.com/

10.   https://www.olympic.org/michael-phelps

THE PROMISE OF LONG TERM RECOVERY

Business

Aaron Swartz

Ben Huh

Elon Musk

Kate Spade

Nidhi Singh

Ted Turner

Composers

Ludwig Van Beethoven

Robert Schumann

Wolfgang Amadeus Mozart

Leaders

Abraham Lincoln

Napoleon Bonaparte

Theodore Roosevelt

Winston Churchill

JOHN FREDERICK ZURN

Musicians

Adam Ant

Axle Rose

Brian Wilson

Britney Spears

Charlie Pride

Gordon Sumner (Sting)

Jimi Hendrix

Mariah Carey

Sinéad O'Connor

Painters

David LaChapelle

Edvard Munch

Gilbert Stuart

Isa Genzken

Jackson Pollock

Kate Millet

Sam Gilliam

Vincent van Gogh

THE PROMISE OF LONG TERM RECOVERY

Scientists
Buzz Aldrin, astronaut
Isaac Newton, mathematician
Florence Nightingale, nursing

117

Television
Dick Cavett
Jane Pauley

A few web sites...
www.realmentalhealth.com/bipolar/bipolar_celebs.asp

www.bphope.com/bipolar-buzz/athletes-stigma-anxiety-depression-bipolar/

www.sartle.com/blog/post/mental-health-art-history-8-artists-with-bipolar-disorder

Novella : Mystery of the Thought Healer

1. A World on The Edge

This is the story of Htrae, an ancient civilization existing at a time when fear and darkness were still in control of the race of mortals. It was a time of selfishness and suffering, when petty dictators wielded their weapons of conquest in order to realize their ruthless ambitions for power. The days of the heroes were now long past; and the beings of this hapless planet were lost in the misery of ignorance and poverty, and all the suffering that these social ills create. Their burdens were many and their opportunities were few.

These impoverished mortals knew only tedious work in the worn out fields or exhausting labor in the dark and dangerous mines. For many, the certainty of their inevitable death was one of the few hopes they dared contemplate. In a perilous land cursed with perpetual moral darkness and utter despair, the time of deliverance was rapidly passing away.

Surprisingly, this downward slide toward the perilous abyss went largely unnoticed by the vast population of mortal beings toiling in this fallen world. Despite their lot, these citizens knew of nothing else, so they grimly accepted their fate. They allowed themselves a small measure of hope that was dishonestly conceived by wicked rulers who engaged in political intrigue. These despots portrayed their dangerous plans as harbingers of peace and worthy of support.

Then, of course, weapons were invented and forged, promising deterrence and protection. Yet, always in the end, when negotiations inevitably failed, wars were declared, and the Htrae world erupted in violence.

With each passing century, the practice of combat became ever more deadly, and millions were sacrificed. Like an unstoppable plague, this obsession with conquest eventually annihilated entire populations and ground the natural world to dust. Now, after centuries of war and the destruction of the natural world, the earth was succumbing to the foul smelling air, the poisonous rivers, and the deforestation of ancient forests.

But it wasn't the conflicts alone ravaging the natural world. Centuries of unregulated commerce and unrestrained science were also to blame for the dire condition of the world. The digging of mines and drilling for oil were responsible too.

Every part of the Htrae world, no matter how remote or pristine, was exploited in order to fill the bank accounts of the wealthy few whose greed and ambition were unquenchable. Science, for its part, tortured the world's most innocent creatures in the name of progress simply to prove their latest theory.

However, there was an ancient prophecy.

Thousands of years earlier, a great sage from the East had predicted this era of darkness and the widespread destruction and despair that would accompany it. This holy man predicted he would return and turn back this tidal wave of war and despair, so the poor would know prosperity and the natural world would be renewed. In the New Age of Light And Love, the behavior of the rich would be noble and compassionate, and the impoverished multitudes would be liberated at last.

After thousands of years, this prophecy had become so tangled with fiction and folklore it had been ultimately relegated to obscure texts and the story teller's campfire. In time, even these sources lost their credibility, and so the words of the "Great Ones" were slowly slipping away. Without the support of even an oral tradition, the legend was in danger of disappearing forever.

There was, however, one fifteen year old girl, Sita, who still believed despite her abject poverty. She was one of the billions of innocent children engulfed by poverty who seemed destined to live a short, miserable life of physical labor; yet she was oblivious to her plight. Fortunately, like most children, she didn't truly understand the hopelessness of her circumstances. In her innocence and charity, she was cheerful, enthusiastic, and eager to help others. Even more admirable was her ability to accept and manage her near deafness which made it difficult for her to communicate with other children.

Instead of feeling sorry for herself, Sita spent her days helping to raise her twin brothers, Jeremy and Adam. She worked tirelessly in the fields with her parents. She was indispensable to her family because of her energetic nature and emotional maturity. Her hard work offered relief, especially for her parents. She did all her chores without being asked and helped Jeremy and Adam with their chores and school work.

Because she could barely hear since birth, Sita had long ago learned the value of books. Safe within their pages, she hid from a mostly silent world that she couldn't understand. The fifteen year old child was eventually able to borrow and read so many books that she was able to imagine an entire universe within her mind. This ability freed her from the indifferent world around her and instilled in her a sense of belonging.

Since she could hear only words and sounds that were spoken very close to her, other children ignored her or sometimes gossiped about her even when she was around them. Since Sita could sometimes read lips, she could understand their conversations, but chose to ignore their insensitivity, and sought out the imaginative companions that she encountered in stories. Over time, she lived more and more within her own world of noble ideas and loving relationships; that was enough for her. Ironically, it was actually through this same fascination with books that Sita rediscovered the lost sage known as the Thought Healer.

2. Sita Meets a Luminous Being

Surprisingly, Sita's understanding of this Great Being didn't come directly from any one book or even from someone else in the village. Instead, the Thought Healer came one day as a kind of vision in which her thoughts and feelings dissolved and were replaced by an emerging light. As Sita watched this extraordinary light with stillness and awareness, a luminous being slowly approached. Sita courageously held her inner gaze on the miraculous image and then the being spoke, "Do not be frightened, my child. You are safe with me. I am very pleased that you have found me in my secret haven behind the Htrae world".

Sita was initially startled when the being began to speak, but his soft words and calming tone convinced her he wasn't a demon or some malevolent ghost.

"Why have you come here to see me?" she asked as her self-confidence returned. "Are you a warrior who has come to conquer the world?"

"No child, I am not". the being replied simply.

"Then who are you, if you don't mind me asking?" Sita continued, becoming more bold.

"I am the Thought Healer, and I'm here to restore Htrae," the being asserted.

"I thought you were only a story," Sita replied in surprise and bewilderment.

"To most, I am a story, or less," answered the Thought Healer. "Yet, you have found me here in my place of seclusion. Now, I am here to help you, but I also need your help as well".

"I'm just a girl," Sita said apprehensively. "I'm not old enough or smart enough to help you. Not only that, I can barely hear. I'm no use to anyone except my family. I don't even know how I can hear you now".

The Thought Healer smiled and the brilliant light surrounding him soon transformed into a rose color with light blue shading. This magnificent radiance was saturated with so much love that it was almost beyond Sita's capacity to bear. When this beautiful light became absorbed back into the mystic's being again.

He said, "Sita, you have been of great assistance to others. It is only because of your service and humility that you haven't thought about the good you've been doing. The very fact that you were able to discover my secret location is proof enough for me that you are capable of helping me".

Sita was still confused and a little unsettled by the Thought Healer's remarks about her life, yet the wondrous vision had also made her more courageous.

"I still don't understand!" she blurted out. "Are you here to help my family and the village?"

The Thought Healer was again impressed with Sita's attitude. Even though she was barely more than a child, she still considered the needs of others instead of her own.

He smiled again at her and answered, "Sita, since you are the only one who has been able to reach me, you must share my burden. With your help, we must rescue your world from those who are unknowingly destroying it".

Sita, who was still unaware of the perils of the outside world, did not comprehend what the Thought Healer was describing.

"What's wrong with the world? Isn't it mostly good? Other children sometimes tease me, but my family loves me".

I know," he replied. "But your views of the world don't extend beyond the village, and your books are mostly stories of adventure with ideas that have no sustainable purpose. You know little about hatred, ambition, and war. Until now, you have been protected. Nevertheless, we have chosen each other for this difficult and dangerous task. So, we must see it through to the end".

THE PROMISE OF LONG TERM RECOVERY

Sita was beginning to feel an uneasy sense of responsibility envelop her now. It was a duty that felt more important than taking care of her brothers or working in the fields with her parents. Suddenly, she felt she was being chosen, not because she was the same as everyone else, but because she was different from them. It was as if a mist was wafting through her mind, and she was seeing clearly for the first time.

"Yes, I will go with you," Sita replied with more self-confidence. "What do you need me to do?"

The Thought Healer spoke even more mysteriously now, as he told Sita about his intended plan.

"You must come back to this place tomorrow at dawn, and don't tell anyone about our meeting. At that time, I will show you many things about our world that you haven't yet discovered. It will be difficult for you. After, we'll talk about the mission. When you leave here today, I will permanently restore your hearing; however, you must pretend that your hearing is the same as before. If your family and the villagers discover the truth, it would bring out emotions in them that you will be compelled to bear".

Sita was so preoccupied by the Thought Healer's appearance and enigmatic words she had forgotten entirely about her deafness. When she finally realized what had happened, her joy and gratitude overwhelmed her, and she began to weep,

"Thank you," she said softly. "I won't let you down, I promise". Then she added hastily, "But I'm still confused. How will I find you? I only found you this time by chance".

"Don't worry," the Thought Healer responded. "I will find you if you come by this stream again at dawn. Now I must go. Remember what I told you".

"Wait!" exclaimed Sita. "I don't even know your name".

"My name is Cadecus," The Thought Healer declared. Then he merged into the dazzling light and disappeared.

The very next moment, Sita heard the world around her clearly for the first time. A symphony of sounds overwhelmed her, as if she had entered a magical realm. Every sound she discovered was now more than a vibration; it was almost a mystical experience. Singing birds in the willows and the sounds of the gurgling stream behind her house became intensely real, as if they were colored fragrance, brimming with a cool intensity. As she scampered through the village, she could hear her family and neighbors chattering away, and her entire world seemed new and fresh like the tangible thrill of twilight.

When Sita finally returned home, she could barely conceal her excitement and enthusiasm, and before long, she forgot about Cadecus's injunction. Her mother was the first to notice the change in her daughter, as she watched Sita skipping across the backyard patio.

"Sita, why you so cheerful?" she asked.

Sita slowed herself down, finally recalling her promise to Cadecus, and resumed her natural attitude of respect and humility. She tried her best to remember how she acted before her near deafness was miraculously healed and replied softly, "It's such a beautiful day, and I just feel happy".

That answer would have been satisfactory if Sita hadn't later made one blatant, yet understandable mistake. While she was cooking supper by the fireplace, her father called from the back patio asking, "Can somebody help me out here?"

Sita immediately turned from the crackling fire and yelled back, "I'll be right there, father!"

3. Sita Learns about Suffering and Death

Sita's mother was stunned by her daughter's sudden ability to hear. She whirled around, stepped over to her, and tapped her gently on the shoulder, exclaiming, "Sita how could you hear what your father was saying? How could you understand him?"

Sita immediately realized her mistake. In the excitement of experiencing her miraculous healing, she had unintentionally revealed her secret; the most important instruction Cadecus had given to her only hours before. Now, if she didn't explain herself satisfactorily, she might lose the chance to accompany the Thought Healer on his mysterious quest. She thought hard for a moment and then a quickly formulated plan arose in her mind. She pulled her notebook from her pocket and wrote down one single word – "What?"

Her mother slowly returned to a calmer state of mind, then gazed at Sita again and asked her about her sudden ability to respond to her father's voice. Sita pretended to be confused and responded, "You know I always talk to myself. Did father say something?"

Sita's response satisfied her mother, but Sita was also deeply saddened by her mother's spontaneous expression of joy that now had been entirely baseless. She gently touched her daughter's chin, and they all went back to their chores.

Sita began to weep silently, and quickly turned away, the moment her mother left her side. She had so wanted to express her joy and reassure her devoted family about her miraculous experience with Cadecus. But somehow she knew that, whatever reasons the Thought Healer had, it was important for her to follow his instructions. So, in order to keep her secret, Sita pretended she couldn't hear at all. As she swept the small four room cottage, however, her sense of curiosity and adventure were slowly awakened once more.

The next day, long before dawn, Sita quietly hurried through her chores. She gathered firewood and filled the clay water jugs at the stream. Then she fed and milked Gana, the family cow. When she was finished, she took one last glance at her home, and sprinted out to the meadow near the hemlock forest.

When she found the rustic stream where she had first met Cadecus, she sat down, calmed herself, and slowed her breathing. She sat quietly for a while, until she could feel her racing thoughts subside. She softly closed her eyes. She gazed within at her thoughts and inner images for several minutes but nothing happened. She maintained her attitude of quiet persistence for several moments more but failed to discern the Thought Healer. Disappointed and frustrated, Sita eventually gave up; however, she remembered Cadecus's mysterious promise that he would find her. She resigned herself to scanning for him in the outer landscape around her; deciding to remain by the stream in silence, patiently awaiting his arrival.

Before long, Sita saw Cadecus standing upstream near the woods. Although barely visible, his long, jet black hair and orange tunic were easily discernable, even at a distance. She immediately jumped up and raced toward him; but as she approached, the Thought Healer seemed to move farther away. After a few minutes, Sita realized that the Great Being was actually leading her into the forest itself.

By the time Sita caught up with Cadecus, she was exhausted, bewildered, and seeking an explanation. Cadecus, however, quickly interrupted and gently scolded her.

"You must learn to follow instructions, child. I can't always explain things to you; you must learn to trust me".

"But my mother seemed so happy and then so disappointed," Sita complained.

"Yes, I know," Cadecus replied. "But I have my reasons. I can't hurry because you're hurrying. Sometimes we must do many things at once".

"I don't understand," Sita complained.

The Thought Healer tried again to explain himself. "Before taking a trip, one must load the wagon and hitch up the oxen, is it not so?"

"Yes," Sita answered, finally understanding. "We have to pack up everything carefully or the trip may not go well".

"That's right," Cadecus replied assuredly. "Patience and faith are important virtues to possess. With that in mind, I have a very important task for you to accomplish. It will also be an important lesson for you to learn as you prepare for our journey".

"What is it?" Sita asked more enthusiastically now.

Cadecus pointed to an outcropping of lichen covered boulders and said, "I want you to walk past those boulders and tell me what you find".

At first, Sita was silent. She was extremely disappointed with the Thought Healer's request, believing Cadecus was sending her on some simple nature hike or childish scavenger hunt. She stared at him coolly and said, "I don't have much time, my parents will be waiting for me".

"Beyond those boulders, there is something you must see," Cadecus replied simply, as he abruptly turned to leave.

The Thought Healer's obscure remark reassured Sita and reignited her curiosity. She dashed up to the huge rocks, crossed over them, and hiked into a gully below. She searched everywhere, anticipating she would make some wonderful discovery or solve some important mystery. But after a while, she began to sense something was very wrong.

In her desire to discover the Thought Healer's secret, she had become lost. The boulders she had crossed over were nowhere to be found; and when she hustled back up the ridge, Cadecus and the stream had vanished as well. A feeling of uncertainty and dread began to grow in Sita's mind until she finally began to panic. Wandering in circles, she realized that she had never been so lost and frightened in her life.

At last, in utter desperation, Sita climbed a gigantic willow tree; there a few miles away, she could barely perceive the outline of a secluded village. At first, it seemed like a tempting mirage, but when the vision remained stable, Sita decided to investigate. From her vantage point, she carefully noted various landmarks that she could employ for finding her way there; odd shaped rock formations and lopsided pine trees. She climbed back down and hurried through the forest, hoping she wouldn't be caught alone in the perilous woods at night.

It was twilight when Sita reached the surprisingly well fortified town. She felt relieved she was finally out of the forest. However, this feeling of security soon abandoned her when she passed through the town's open gate. As she looked around, she thought it peculiar that a village surrounded by such formidable walls should have a wide open entrance. Yet when she passed through the entrance and walked onto the cobblestone street, Sita understood why the gate was unattended.

Everyone in the town appeared to be dead. In the street, people of all ages were lying in rigid grotesque positions with strange sores oozing from their bodies and faces.

In front of every house and shop, there were dead bodies sprawled out on the sidewalk, as if they had just fallen down dead where they stood. Bodies were stacked up like wood at both the church and livery stable. The only prominent signs on the buildings were red crosses on doors and windows. The faces of the dead appeared to be panic stricken or tormented. Worst of all was the stench. The smell of rotting corpses contaminated the air, encouraging the squabbling turkey vultures attracted by the foul decay.

Sita was terrified and incredulous. She wasn't entirely certain what had happened to these poor dead beings; but she knew she couldn't help them now. As she walked to the far edge of the town, the awful stench of death became even more poignant. Sita reluctantly decided to find out why. Covering her nose with her sleeve, she walked toward the awful smell and discovered over a dozen wagons loaded with the diseased remains of both children and adults. As she forced herself to move past them, she soon encountered a gigantic pit with bodies littered at the bottom or snagged against the jagged dirt walls. She turned in horror; not knowing what to do, she returned to the disease infested village.

As twilight gave way to darkness, Sita stared at the dead bodies trying to understand what had occurred. She lit a torch and couldn't decide whether it was more dangerous to remain in the village or face the uncertainties of the night forest. While she was brooding over her situation, she heard the unmistakable sound of a boy calling out to her. She immediately turned following the voice, until suddenly a boy appeared from behind a building. When he drew closer, Sita stood still, not knowing what to do. The boy seemed puzzled as well and waited for her to make the first move.

Before long, Sita's compassionate nature asserted itself. She approached the boy and embraced him. His clothes were filthy - little more than rags. There were scars all over his neck. Sita overlooked the boy's condition. She was so relieved to find another living soul that she held him for a long time. The young boy soon began weeping and slowly let his emotions spill out. After a few moments, Sita asked him, "What is your name?"

"My name is Dukka," the boy answered. "I'm the only one left".

"My name is Sita. What happened here?"

The boy spoke haltingly as he told Sita about the dreadful events he had witnessed. "This spring, a group of soldiers from the city of Galaway arrived in our village, and they all spent a week hunting in the nearby forests. On the fourth day of their visit, the village physician realized that the soldiers had all contracted a terrible sickness called the Crimson Plague. When the doctor informed the mayor, the mayor panicked, and both he and the physician fled from our village in the middle of the night. By the time the villagers discovered the truth, many of them had become infected. It wasn't long before the soldiers and all the villagers either fled or died".

"What about you?" Sita asked slowly, trying to comprehend the horror of the plague. "Why aren't you sick?"

Dukka was silent for a very long time and finally replied, "I was sick, terribly sick. But I didn't die like the others because the plague left me after a few days. In the entire village, I am the only survivor. Now you must go".

Sita was very confused and somewhat frightened by Dukka's account of the Crimson Plague. But, she knew she would never forgive herself if she left the boy behind. She needed to convince him to trust her.

"I can't go into the forest alone again, she asserted diplomatically, and you can't stay here with all this terrible disease and death. I'm not staying here and neither are you. "Now please lead us through the forest".

At first, Dukka refused, fearing for Sita's safety. Then he realized Sita might actually abandon him if he remained in the village, so he ultimately agreed to accompany her.

He took charge and began guiding them both through the dense pine forest and treacherous thickets. As they pressed on, Dukka finally related to Sita their destination. "We must travel to Galaway," he asserted confidentially. "It is a magnificent city with many rich nobles and clever healers. We must find out more about the Crimson Plague that wiped out my village and nearly killed me".

"Why?" Sita asked innocently. "You're all right now, and there is no one else to save".

"Except you," Dukka replied.

It was only then that Sita finally understood the terrible risk she had taken by entering the village. In her little town, people got hurt or sick and even died, but they never died in large numbers or even in the same way. For the first time in her life, Sita understood the concept of death as a cataclysmic event. She shook with fear when she realized that she, herself, could have actually contracted this terrifying disease that was most probably fatal.

THE PROMISE OF LONG TERM RECOVERY

Despite her trepidation; Sita was able to consider Dukka's situation more clearly as well. She began to understand he was a very unusual child. Even though he had lost both his parents and had barely survived the Crimson Plague, Dukka was still able to express compassion and concern for her even though he barely knew her. As Sita's panic of contracting the disease gradually subsided, she hiked behind her young friend until dawn. Then, after a brief respite, they made their way toward Galaway.

By the time they reached the small villages surrounding Galaway, it was midmorning, and evidence of the plague was everywhere. Businesses and cottages were boarded up and locked from the outside. Only the very ill and the dead were visible on the streets and in the alleys. Foul smelling corpses were piled behind the livery stable and in front of the churches. Vermin were free to scurry around unchallenged. It sickened Sita to witness such suffering and stench. But she followed Dukka anyway, as he cautiously eluded the grasp of the dying, pleading for help. He understood that these poor souls were dead already. He and Sita hurried on ignoring their awful cries. At last, a number of square two story structures appeared directly ahead. They realized they had reached their destination - the metropolis of Galaway.

When they had reached the outskirts of the city, Sita and Dukka were almost immediately accosted by an exceedingly tall soldier standing guard at the massive gate. Although the guard appeared fearless, when he first spoke, his tone revealed a feeling of weariness and dread.

"Who are you and what do you want?" the guard bellowed attempting to sound threatening.

"I am Dukka and this is my friend, Sita," the boy responded cautiously. "We have come to speak with your physicians about the plague. We are seeking a cure".

The melancholy guard suddenly started to laugh and blurted out, "Cure? What cure? Everyone is sick! If there were a cure, don't you think we would have already given it to the sick and dying?"

"Could we just talk with a doctor?" Dukka continued pressing his point.

"Look!" the guard answered angrily, losing his patience. "Nobody is allowed in or out of the city and that includes you two presumptuous children!"

Dukka and Sita were initially very disappointed, but when they turned away from the gate, the guard did something completely unexpected. He groaned piteously and fell down dead. Astonished, they stared down at the old man. Sita chose to interpret his death as an omen. She was once again overwhelmed by the plague's cruelty. She couldn't comprehend how a person could be standing one moment and be dead on the ground a moment later. Confusion and fear swept through her mind; she was overcome with distress.

Dukka recovered his composure more quickly having grown accustomed to the horror of the plague in his own village. Unlike Sita, he realized the guard's death provided them an opportunity to pass through the gate and into the city. He grabbed her hand, and hurriedly jogged down the cobblestone streets, passing under the dilapidated structures which served as shops and residences.

As in Dukka's village, the shadow of death was dark and deep. Every doorway and street corner was strewn with dead bodies. Crows feasting on human and animal remains. The scene closely resembled the aftermath of a battlefield or natural disaster with no one remaining alive to bury the dead.

As they searched diligently for any physician's office, Dukka and Sita began to discern that some citizens were actually still very much alive. It appeared that they had either locked themselves in the upper rooms of various residences to keep others out, or had been forcibly locked in and couldn't escape. There were even some unfortunate souls concealing themselves behind boxes and barrels in the cellars of these plague ridden buildings.

As they hurried along with uncertainty and alarm, Sita and Dukka finally located a physician's shingle hanging above a half opened door. They both immediately stepped inside, startling a man behind the counter who was making a foul smelling potion.

"Are you a doctor?" Dukka asked.

"Yes I am," the man proclaimed.

He was shabbily dressed. It appeared he hadn't bathed for at least a week. There was an unmistakable sense of desperation in his pale face that he tried to conceal. "I'm the doctor," he repeated. "How can I help you?"

Sita sensed that the man's attempt to appear relaxed was not merely a ruse, so she decided to challenge him.

"Sir," she asked, "How are you treating this illness that has stricken the citizens of Galaway?"

The man muttered some incoherent words repeatedly and then, unexpectedly, sat down and began to weep.

"I know this is not my office and I'm trespassing," he sobbed miserably. "But the real physicians have all died or run off, and my wife is very ill. All our children have been taken, only my wife and I remain. I'm trying to save her life. Please don't have me arrested".

Sita was deeply moved by the man's distress and devotion, as she watched the tears trickle down his grief stricken face. However, she was also becoming aware that their own search for a cure might be beyond their grasp. After considering the situation carefully, Sita concluded her only hope of survival now was to remain healthy. That strategy didn't seem very realistic especially considering the circumstances.

After seeing the man's agony, Sita decided to comfort him and take on the burden of caring for his wife. "What's your name?" Sita asked sweetly. "And who is your wife?"

"My name is Peter, miss," he answered. "And my wife is Ella".

"All right" Sita answered. "Now, take me to your home," Sita directed.

Peter walked out of the physician's office, into the street, while Dukka and Sita followed close behind. As they turned the corner, they suddenly became aware of hysterical townspeople banging on doors and windows from inside various cottages and shops. They immediately stopped and asked Peter to explain this startling scene which they themselves had briefly witnessed when they first arrived in Galaway.

"Who is locked up in all these buildings?" Sita yelled out.

Peter stopped only long enough to explain. "If someone gets sick in any building, they lock everyone inside".

Sita was dumfounded. "Are you saying that if anyone in a building is infected, everyone else is locked up with them?"

"Yes," Peter responded more impatiently. "It helps control the spread of the contagion".

"But it doesn't," Dukka replied simply. "Almost everyone dies no matter what precautions are taken".

Dukka's remarks moved Sita deeply. She felt the need to respond to the anguished cries of the imprisoned citizens all around her. She decided to find a way to unbolt all the structures regardless of who was in them. When they reached Peter's house, Sita agreed to help Ella; however, she also directed Peter and Dukka to open all the condemned buildings and set the captives free who were locked inside. They both reluctantly agreed. Peter was very frightened and uneasy as he said goodbye to his wife.

As soon as they were gone, Sita went to Ella's bedside and tried to comfort her with cold compresses, sips of water, and compassionate words. In only a matter of hours, however, with Peter and Dukka still somewhere in the city; Ella's health quickly deteriorated and death was fast approaching. Sita made one last attempt to reassure her.

"Ella, soon you will be free from your pain and suffering. Then this illness will no longer have any power over you. Your troubles will be over".

Ella smiled weakly, then took her last few agonizing breaths, and said, "But now your troubles have just begun".

Ella's cryptic remarks surprised and puzzled Sita. She stared at Ella's lifeless body in bewildered silence. However, before long, she understood the meaning of Ella's prophetic words. As she turned to leave the room, she discovered a stinging sensation originating on her forehead and felt a grotesquely shaped nodule throbbing against her irritated neck. She stood completely still, shocked and disorientated, and fled from the house in horror.

Sita rushed into the street in despair nearly stumbling over the dead and dying scattered everywhere on the ground. In a state of utter panic, she shrieked out Dukka's name frantically searching the city for Peter and her friend. Almost immediately, she became light headed and nauseated, the buildings around her seemed to spin. She collapsed on the ground, delirious from the fever infecting her mind and body.

Fortunately, Dukka and Peter heard Sita's anguished cries for help and rushed to her side. They tried to comfort her, but she was too feeble to appear grateful. Instead, her voice was strained, her strength quickly abandoning her.

Peter, moved by Sita's plight, was also very concerned about his wife's well being. He couldn't resist asking Sita about her.

"Sita," he asked hesitantly, "How is my Ella?"

In her suffering and alarm, Sita had completely forgotten about Ella. She was now so ill; she was much more concerned for her own survival. "She's dead, Peter. I'm sorry".

"What!" Peter cried out angrily. "My wife died and I wasn't there! You had me helping everyone else instead. I should have been with Ella and not breaking into plague infected buildings!"

"I'm sorry, Peter," Sita answered weakly. "You're right. What good is it to help everyone else if you can't be with your own family?"

To his credit, however, it didn't take long for Peter to realize the truth for himself. He knew Ella was already dead before he left . He now felt certain that Sita had done all she could. "Come on, Dukka," Peter said with a feeling of resignation. "We must find a place for Sita to rest.

Peter and Dukka picked her up their dying friend and carried her down the street until they reached an empty basement. They laid her down on the cold musty floor. It was only then that Sita finally remembered the Thought Healer.

"Cadecus! Cadecus!" she cried out in desperation. "Where are you?"

When the Thought Healer failed to answer Sita's desperate cry for help, Peter and Dukka were unable to offer her with any consolation. Her terrible suffering had overwhelmed her courage, and her thoughts were dark and disjointed. Her condition continued to worsen. Since Peter knew he couldn't ease her mind, he left Dukka alone with her while he departed to bury his wife.

When Peter had gone, Dukka spoke. "My child, still you don't recognize me?"

Sita gave Dukka a terrified glance. In her suffering and distress, she couldn't understand her friend's inexplicable words. Finally, the enigmatic stranger touched Sita's forehead, and they were both transported back to the stream near the outcropping of boulders.

Sita immediately recognized the familiar landscape and quickly examined her forehead and neck. The fever and nodule were gone. She gazed intently at Dukka, and saw him miraculously transform into the Great Being - Cadecus.

At first, Sita was reassured by the Thought Healer's presence, but soon became angry and defensive. "Why did you try to kill me?" Sita demanded. "You told me I needed to learn about life from you. Does that include terrifying me and nearly murdering me?"

Cadecus was silent for a while allowing Sita to express her indignation. He also remained quiet to give her the opportunity to answer her own question. Finally, he was compelled to respond.

"Sita," he began slowly, "The word "Dukka' means suffering and it's a part of life. In fact, it isn't possible to learn about suffering without experiencing it yourself. The same is true of death. It cannot be adequately understood by merely witnessing it in others. It is a solitary experience. There is another reason for learning about both suffering and death. It is the best way for you to learn compassion for the plight of others".

Sita was still distressed even after hearing the Thought Healer's explanation; her anger still apparent in her tone.

"I'm going home now," she stated bluntly. "I don't wish to learn anything more from you. Besides, I'm already very late, and my family will be worried. This lesson has been a waste of time".

"Where is time?" Cadecus asked rhetorically.

Sita departed from the Thought Healer and ran all the way home. When she arrived, she raced inside the small cottage and hugged her father warmly. He looked at her kindly and said, "Thanks for feeding the cows and fetching the water. You were up before I was this morning!"

Her father's remark both surprised and startled Sita. She gazed around the cottage carefully and suddenly realized that she had been gone for only a few hours.

4. The Enchanted Notebook

Sita was greatly reassured by her loving family. She felt a renewed sense of security. Her short, intense encounter with Cadecus by the stream, and her strange experiences in the forest left her puzzled and frightened. Now these troubles were behind her. Safely together with her family once more; she enthusiastically attended to her daily chores and allowed herself to relax. Her daily routine provided a powerful source of comfort and support. Her terrifying ordeal slowly lost its hold over her. Allowing her dreadful memories to fade, Sita embraced her old life as if it were fresh and exciting.

Sita also resolved to inform her parents about Cadecus and his miraculous ability to cure her deafness. Her mother especially deserved to hear the truth. She carried the burden of worry and guilt that she couldn't always conceal from her daughter. Sita also decided to describe her horrifying experiences with the Crimson Plague including her near fatal illness in Galaway.

For about a week, Sita waited patiently for an opportunity to tell her parents when they were alone. At last, she found them together, in the barn gathering straw, while her brothers Adam and Jeremy were still asleep.

"You were right, mother," Sita began enthusiastically. "Now, I _can_ hear. But I wasn't supposed to tell you".

Her parents stopped what they were doing and looked at their daughter in amazement.

Her mother asked, "Sita, did you say you can hear?"

Sita nodded enthusiastically and backed about thirty yards away from them. "Say something!" she shouted.

Her father hesitated at first, but then began to recite the letters of the alphabet in a random order. Sita miraculously repeated them all correctly.

Sita's mother cried out, "Sita, oh my Sita," and hurried to embrace her.

Her father also became very inspired, but he was also perplexed. "How can this be?" he asked when he caught up with her.

"It's really hard to explain," Sita began. "And it's even more difficult to believe".

"Go on," her mother encouraged. "We need to know".

"All right," Sita replied, drawing a deep breath. "While I was hiking through the forest, I met a Thought Healer named Cadecus".

Before Sita could continue, her father interrupted her. "What's a Thought Healer?"

Sita's mother quickly interrupted him. "Keep still! Let her finish! Go on Sita".

"Anyway," Sita went on. "First, Cadecus came to me in a kind of dream vision. Later, I met him in person by the giant boulders near the stream behind our farm. While I was there, he tricked me into disappearing into another world where everyone was sick".

While Sita continued to relate her highly improbable story, it became clear that her parents were becoming confused and frightened. She soon discerned that she couldn't tell them the truth; if she did, they might consider her to be mentally unstable needing careful supervision. So, she decided to bend the truth for everyone's sake.

"What I'm trying to say," she said meekly, "is that it was like a beautiful dream. When I finally woke up, I could hear".

Sita's parents' expression of relief and elation gave Sita all the evidence required to understand that her parents had been persuaded.

"It's a miracle!" her mother exclaimed. "Who would have thought our little girl could be healed in a dream? It's a miracle!"

Within hours Sita was a noteworthy person in her tiny village. Her father was especially proud, repeating the story, embellishing it every time he told it. Sita was now free to be herself. She drank in all the wonderful sounds and songs that now filled her mind and touched her heart.

Nevertheless, despite her good fortune and her best efforts, Sita still couldn't get Cadecus out of her thoughts. Days drifted into months. She still replayed the entire plague incident in her mind; attempting to put it to rest, so she could move beyond it. However, her experiences had been complicated and rendered no clear or simple explanations. Although Cadecus had tricked her, he had also miraculously improved her hearing. Just as important, he had come to her in a magic vision. If he were evil, how could he heal her and create such a wondrous light?

It became clear after several months of inner turmoil that Sita simply couldn't answer her own questions. She needed to contact the Thought Healer himself if she was going to find the answers she was so earnestly seeking. So one afternoon, with this belief directing her steps, Sita approached the meandering stream near her home and sat down. She was determined to wait for Cadecus in the exact spot where they had first met. From her vantage point, she could see her parents sitting in front of their thatched cottage oblivious to her movements. The wafting smoke from the stone chimney indicated her brothers were napping, and her parents would soon be preparing dinner.

As she lingered by the stream, Sita wrote down all the questions she would ask Cadecus when he appeared, carefully rehearsing each one out loud. While she waited, the time dragged on, her courage and fervor waned. She soon became dejected believing another encounter with Cadecus was highly improbable.

But then he appeared. He was such a unique and mysterious being, Sita could have recognized him from a great distance; yet the Thought Healer chose to appear directly behind her, near the forest pines. Soon he was beside her.

"Cadecus!" Sita exclaimed forgetting her carefully crafted questions. "You're really here! I knew you'd come!" The Thought

Healer's presence both inspired and invigorated Sita. She felt the thrill of adventure returning.

"Yes," Cadecus answered in a calm resolute voice. "I have come to answer your questions and ask one of my own".

Sita suddenly remembered her notes and decided to ask her two most important questions. "Cadecus," she said tentatively. "Why did you lead me into those awful places of death and disease when you disguised yourself as Dukka?"

"If you want to travel with me," Cadecus answered, "you must be aware that suffering is a part of life. It's not possible to truly learn about sorrow without experiencing it, as I have already told you. Since you, and most others, wouldn't actively seek out suffering to understand it, I decided to bring it to you. It was a kind of initiation, designed to test your courage and patience. By giving you the most difficult challenge first, I will now be able to teach you more quickly. Instead of assigning you some small, largely inconsequential assignments first, I simply created one very challenging test so you could prove yourself. Now, what is your other question?"

Sita was beginning to understand the Thought Healer a little better even if she didn't agree with him. She decided to ask her second question. "Why did you advise me to hide your hearing miracle from my family?"

"You already know the answer," Cadecus replied slowly. "What happened when you told your parents about me?"

"I think they thought I was mentally unstable," Sita admitted.

"Yes, if you would've continued relating your honest description," the Thought Healer continued, "everyone would have ridiculed you or worse. Your clever response about the dream was quite resourceful. That kind of quick thinking could prove useful in the future. Now I have a question for you. Why is it you only called for me when you were dying? Why didn't you seek me out when the others were dying?"

The truth of the Thought Healer's statement stung Sita's pride, and she instantly realized the truth. She bowed her head and replied, "Even though I helped others, I didn't treat their suffering as my own. I could have called you at any time and ended all our anguish".

Cadecus smiled and realized his trust was well placed in his young student. "Yes, it is so. Thoughts of selfishness can be extremely subtle and very difficult to overcome. The most important thing is that you did learn from your mistake, and that you have ultimately overcome your fear. It is also true you helped others throughout the entire episode.

"Sita, to be honest," the Thought Healer continued more seriously now. "I need your complete cooperation. Your good ideas and noble actions will not be enough even though they are truly important. Every situation we will soon encounter will have many unknown dangers requiring a combination of courage, resourcefulness and charity. I must prepare you myself or our mission will fail. It is concern, not harshness, motivating me to create these reflective visions".

Sita tried to understand Cadecus's strange clarification. She felt inclined to believe him, at least enough to begin to trust him again. She sat in silence for only a few moments, then with both fear and anticipation, asked the Thought Healer about her task.

"I'm ready to try again," she called out, attempting to sound both modest and confident.

Cadecus felt a sense of solace realizing that Sita might indeed be the one for whom he had been searching. He bent down and picked up her green notebook laying on the ground beside her, toring out all the pages except three. Returning it to her, Sita held it in her hands and watched in amazement, as it began to twinkle with an ethereal blue glow. It felt very cool to her touch, and soon began emitting a whirring sound that created a feeling of strength. While Sita continued grasping the glowing notebook, Cadecus touched it with a quick "rap" and the notebook returned to its original color and texture.

THE PROMISE OF LONG TERM RECOVERY

Before Sita could recover from her surprise long enough to ask questions, the Thought Healer explained. "Since I crafted the first challenge, I am giving you the chance to create the second one. Your assignment is to write an original story. It must be started at dawn and completed by sunset. In other words, you must continue writing until you succeed in composing your narrative in a single day.

"Why?" Sita interrupted, already complaining. "Anyone can write a story".

Cadecus raised his voice sternly and replied, "Your impatience is still a problem. You didn't allow me to finish. This composition is not to be just any story. Whatever story you write between the hours of dawn and twilight will become true on the following day".

"I don't understand," Sita said, more respectfully now.

"You must write a three page story," Cadecus continued authoritatively, "and you must begin to write at dawn and finish by sunset. When the task is completed the story will come to life the following day".

Having understood Cadecus's explanation in more detail, Sita realized this was the kind of challenge she might truly enjoy. She would be the one inventing the characters and plot. She could compose a "happy ending" that didn't involve death, disease, or despair. She could even make certain no unforeseen forces were lurking behind rocks and trees.

As she held her enchanted notebook more respectfully now, as if it were a sacred text or living presence, she still wished to ask her mysterious guide two more important questions. "What if I can't complete the story in a single day?" she wanted to know". What will happen?"

The Thought Healer gazed down at the stream and replied enigmatically, "Then you will grow old trying".

It was only then that Sita understood the importance of her new task beyond its novelty and her childish thoughts of wish fulfillment.

She vowed to herself she would write the most hopeful, promising story she could. As she studied the notebook again, it became clear this writing task would be more complicated than she had first believed. Like an arrow shot from a bow, it couldn't be recalled once in motion. This grim realization about her writing assignment created a feeling of doubt and responsibility which she initially thought she might escape. When she looked up to ask Cadecus about these forebodings filling her mind, he was gone.

5. A Test of Faith

Sita walked home that day feeling a sense of urgency about her unusual writing project. She entered through the back door. Attempting to project a casual attitude, she greeted her parents cheerfully. She climbed the stairs to her room and hid her notebook among her sweaters in the dresser's bottom drawer. At dinner, she behaved as if nothing out of the ordinary was going on. She returned to her room as soon as she could leave the table without arousing suspicion. That night, as she laid in her bed unable to sleep, her wild and wandering thoughts attempted to create a magical story.

Initially, to be sure, Sita's thoughts betrayed her immaturity. She thought of galloping princes and magnificent castles. She entertained ideas taken from children's books such as the granting of three wishes and the appearance of a magic carpet. Even still, something deep within her heart prompted her to write something more compelling than a selfish and naive story.

Sita ultimately began to focus her attention on the needs of others - helping the sick, the lonely, or even the dying. She began to consider that Cadecus would be impressed with her if she could demonstrate a genuine wish to help those in distress.

But then another thought began to pull at her. Wasn't the desire to please Cadecus just another form of selfishness? Clearly, she was self-centered if her primary reason for writing a story was ultimately to impress her mentor, the Thought Healer.

This feeling of being limited by the constraints of her childish story ideas left Sita feeling restless and worried until almost daybreak. Frustrated and fatigued, she finally decided to get out of bed early and complete her chores as quickly as prudence would allow. Then she hurried up to her room and retrieved the notebook from its hiding place. After taking a few deep breaths, she centered herself and began to write. It was lunch time before Sita took a break. As she read over the first two pages, she felt satisfied that her story was progressing smoothly and rapidly.

After careful consideration, Sita had resolved to write about the beauty of the natural world around her. Having experienced the pain of suffering and disease, the young writer now wished to describe the more elegant scenes of the transforming seasons. If the world was sometimes harsh, it could be beautiful too.

Yet Sita also understood that once she had finished her nature story, she would have to be willing to face both the intended and unintended consequences of her work regardless of her good intentions. Nevertheless, she was determined. Cadecus had given her the responsibility of writing a story, and she would faithfully follow his instructions.

The first full day of Sita's writing project went well; but she was unable to finish because she couldn't create a character to fit her ideas. The next two days were frustrating, because her parents needed her to help thatch the roof, weed the vegetable garden, and make supper. Finally, after a number of interruptions and near completions, Sita eventually completed the writing task in a single day. As the shadows of evening slowly enveloped her room, she hid the completed story under her pillow, waiting eagerly for the rising sun to magically bring her composition to li

At dawn, the incredible happened. Sita and the rest of her family were rudely awakened by a sharp rap at the front door. Sita's father was the first to vault out of bed and respond to the strange knock. When he opened the door, he was shocked to discover a sad old man humbly stretching out his dry withered hand begging for something to eat. Sita raced to the door next and saw the very being she had written about in her story. She approached him more closely and asked. "Are you Father Time?"

"Yes," he replied weakly. "I am very old, and very, very tired. I need to rest for a while."

In her naivety, Sita had written herself into her story, as a temporary replacement for Father Time believing she could portray the wondrous beauty of the seasons in her story. "I will take charge for a while," she said eagerly. "You can rest by the fire for three days, and then you can take over again".

"Very well," Father Time said meekly. "If it's all right with you, I'll rest by the fire now."

Just as Sita's story had foretold, her family granted Father Time's request and left the old man alone by the fire after he had eaten. This gave Sita the chance to assume her primary roles as writer and director. She stepped outside with the purity of good intentions and the predicament of adolescence, and began to transform the season of summer to winter. The young creator raised her arms and began to powder the willows and pines with white fluffy snow. She then froze the meandering stream into a sheet of transparent ice that glowed in the sun. She even cloaked the cottages and streets with a thick layer of beautiful crystal snowflakes.

The unsuspecting villagers were stunned by the drastic change of the landscape around them, and at first were awestruck. The wondrous display of natural forces seemed like a miracle. But before long, the sobering reality of their situation began to take hold. Every part of their natural world was now either sleeping or dying, the vegetables and fruits freezing on the vines and trees. The frigid icy wind assaulted them where they stood; they worriedly gathered firewood and sought shelter from the storm.

But that wasn't the worst of it. Sita's brothers, Adam and Jeremy, had accidentally fallen into a deep pool in the village stream at the exact moment it had frozen, and now they were both motionless at th

By the time Sita realized her brothers deadly peril, she was understandably alarmed. Racing to find her notebook to discover what had happened, she was horrified to find it was gone. Searching everywhere, at last she figured out what might have happened. Her brothers must have been snooping in her room and pilfered her secret notebook. They must also have scribbled something down while she was busy with her chores. Bolting to their room, she found the story book. Turning to the back cover, there indeed were two sketched stick figures with her brothers' names, Adam and Jeremy, scrawled at the bottom. The drawing appeared to show her brothers holding their breath beneath the surface of the ice-covered water.

It was long past time to tell her parents the truth. Searching for them in a complete panic, she finally found them in the barn. She hysterically tried to explain the whole crisis including the magic notebook. She also blurted out the details about the life threatening condition of her brothers who were imprisoned in the frozen stream. She even showed them the stick figure drawings on the bottom of the notebook itself.

Unfortunately, her parents didn't understand her. "What are you talking about Sita?" her mother asked. "You don't have any brothers. Show your father your book".

Her father seemed unconcerned as well. "You know you are an only child, Sita. But it would be nice if you had a couple of brothers, wouldn't it? Now, help your mother bring in some firewood, this blizzard is getting worse.

"Oh, no!" Sita gasped silently, finally realizing her terrible mistake. "I forgot to write Adam and Jeremy into my story, so they decided to write themselves into it. What have I done?"

Sita tried desperately to gain control over her racing thoughts and endeavored to consider the situation more rationally. She then suddenly remembered, Father Time, sleeping by the fire. She raced inside but on approaching him, found he was so deeply asleep that he was impossible to wake. Her panic intensified when she attempted to return the winter season to summer and failed. Her story required three days of winter, and it was now only the first afternoon. The young author was frightened beyond all consolation, even as her parents attempted to make sense of their daughter's strange conversation and behavior.

At last, the terrified girl shouted out for Cadecus; so he could break the spell, but this time he didn't respond. She called repeatedly until finally she realized she would have to restore the situation herself. Then, like a miracle, the truth about the crisis finally eased her tortured mind. In two days, everything would return to the way it had been. She need only patiently wait.

Sita's conclusion was plausible, but time passed with agonizing slowness, keeping her in a perpetual state of doubt and fear. When she finally awoke on the third day, the experience seemed like some horrible nightmare. She immediately rushed into her brothers' room and found them peacefully sleeping. She could find no evidence of harm to either of them and neither could she find Father Time. She was also greatly relieved that her parents were not aware of her exceedingly poor judgment.

With gratitude and relief, Sita sprinted out to the village stream where she and Cadecus had met, the troublesome notebook safely tucked under her arm. Several hours later the Thought Healer appeared, seeming very disappointed. "That was an odd story you wrote," he said sternly. "Did you deliberately leave your brothers out?"

"No, Cadecus," Sita stammered. "I didn't want them to get hurt. But I guess I mostly just forgot about them."

"Yes," Cadecus replied. "If I hadn't remained with them for those three days, they would have perished."

"I don't understand". Sita answered, suddenly anxious again. "My story lasted three days and then it was over."

"That is true," Cadecus asserted. "But just because your story lasted three days doesn't mean those days didn't exist at all. Reality is much more complicated than you realize.

"I still don't understand," the girl spoke in confusion.

"I was required to restore everything you altered as if it never occurred," the Thought Healer replied. "I wanted you to experience the consequences of your lack of self-discipline in writing about things that affect others."

Sita was finally beginning to understand. "Does that mean you were Father Time in my story?" she asked.

"I am part of everyone and everything," Cadecus replied. "It is important to remember that nothing stands alone. Everything is affected by everything else. You must consider that it is as important to remember what you've left out of your life, as it is to remember what you've put into it. Like your brothers, for instance. You also neglected to consider how your story might affect the villagers."

Sita, exhausted from her ordeal, and was seeking rest and forgiveness from the Thought Healer. Although she had made mistakes, they weren't deliberate.

Cadecus's face softened a bit, seeing his student struggling, "Remember child, mistakes, even innocent ones, can be dangerous and even deadly. Even good intentions can lead to disaster."

"Yes," Sita replied grateful that Cadecus still cared for her. Carefully returning the notebook to the Thought Healer, she was clearly relieved to be free of the responsibility.

But instead of accepting it, Cadecus tapped the notebook, allowed the story to dissolve, and returned it to her saying, "Try again, child."

6. The Final Audition

At first, Sita was unwilling to even consider the idea the Thought Healer was proposing. The very thought of writing another mysterious narrative terrified her. "I will not," she uttered in a tone revealing both anger and apprehension. "You told me yourself that I didn't write a story that was useful to any

"I disagree," Cadecus replied with a measure of understanding in his voice. "The story may not have helped others, but it did help you to better understand yourself and the world ar

Sita was still not inclined to be persuaded by the Thought Healer's argument this time. She correctly inferred he was endeavoring to persuade her to participate in yet another test. These tests were supposed to be preparing her for some mission yet seemed pointless and even cruel. Suddenly, again, Cadecus surprised her. "This will be your final challenge. This world is in desperate need of our service, so I've been required to teach you as quickly and intensely as possible. I apologize for your rather rough treatment, but it was una

The young girl, now more willing to listen to the Thought Healer's words, was still badly shaken, vividly remembering her failures. But a moment later, Sita shared a revelation of her own. "I will write another story," she began, "if I can cast you as a main character. Then, whenever I need you, you will be right beside

Cadecus admired the girl's growing shrewdness and attention to detail. With him by her side, he knew that she believed that the plot and themes of her story would be far less likely to twist and turn in dangerous directions. He was inclined to grant her request, but added one more element. "If I am going to travel with you, your story must be filled with real risks and challenges, otherwise it will not teach you anything worth learning. Our mission is about to begin, so finish the story quickly. Then, I can reveal to you my true identity and the purpose of our journey. Now go, child, and return s

Sita returned to her family cottage. Adam and Jeremy were playing in the yard. Her parents were working in the field. Almost instinctively, she grabbed a hoe, joining her parents in their work, still musing about the Thought Healer's enigmatic remarks. She'd been badly frightened twice, and yet still agreed to another difficult assignment. She had detected a sense urgency in his voice - both eerie and distur

Yet, the young student also felt a profound sense of duty toward Cadecus and his mission. She decided to draft the story as quickly as possible. This sense of responsibility included planning the entire plot ahead of time, so she could recreate it from memory. Then she could be assured that her chances for success would be greatly enhanced.

It seemed even Providence itself was guiding Sita. Her parents and twin brothers were scheduled to visit her mother's friend overnight. Sita's parents needed her to complete all the chores while they were away. This fortunate circumstance would allow the young writer to work at the kitchen table and finishing the chores during short breaks. By the time her family was ready to depart a few hours later, Sita was so enthusiastic that she nearly pushed them out the front

Finally alone, Sita took out the mysterious notebook from its new hiding place behind the kitchen cupboard and began to write. She transcribed her thoughts all day stopping just long enough to complete her chores. By twilight, she had completed her task. Sita was so tired and the story so occupied her mind, that she nodded off to sleep, resting her head on the kitchen table. At dawn, came another cryptic knock on the door. Sita, opening the door slightly, peeked out. She yelled, "Cadecus you're h

"Yes, Sita, I am with you now. So let's begin your story. It's called "The Wizard Girl of Waterville" is it

"Yes," the writer beamed. "I think you'll like

The two companions, student and master, left the cottage, walking toward the winding village stream near the woods. Upon reaching its banks, they turned around a bend along its narrow shoreline. Then, unexpectedly, the entire countryside was utterly transformed. The sky was now filled with dark ominous clouds and the ground saturated by a cold steady rain. Stronger than a misty drizzle, the rain fell relentlessly. Only a few rays of sunlight penetrated the massive cloud cover above t

Continuing along the river bank, Cadecus and Sita reached a tiny village with about two dozen structures. They appeared to be businesses, local government offices, and small residential dwellings. There was almost no one in the street; the atmosphere felt as cold and uninviting as the weat

Seeking to escape the deluge, Cadecus and Sita ducked inside a nearby general store, introducing themselves to the proprietor, standing behind a long wooden counter. Surprisingly, the solitary man didn't respond with either warmth or civility. The arrogant sulking fellow appeared totally indifferent to their every attempt at friendly conversation. Sita, discreetly glancing at the other patrons in the store, observed they were equally unfriendly, their accusing eyes and angry scowls making her feel like a criminal.

Sita, of course, anticipated this encounter, but its intensity surprised her. She began to worry about the merits of her unfolding story. Nevertheless, she decided to allow the plot to unfold as written. Waiting patiently a few moments longer, she observed an old woman hobbling into the shop.

The aged woman, frail and bent over, had cold piercing eyes. Intent upon examining every item in the shop, the old woman wandered down every aisle, making the owner and other patrons very uneasy. Before long, the customers, so genuinely intimidated by her presence, began exiting the shop as quickly and discreetly as possible.

As Sita continued to study the old woman lurking around the aisles. She began to identify more of the character's traits from her story. In addition to the old woman's strange appearance and intense gaze, she mumbled angrily to herself, as if cursing at someone or something. This spectacle, suggesting a sense of mental instability, appeared both suspicious and ominous. The old woman continued this odd behavior for the entire time she was in the shop, picking up various items and putting them back down. Eventually, she chose some vegetables and fruit, leaving the place as menacingly as she had arrived. After she was gone, the customers quickly reentered the shop and began cursing the old woman under their breath, so softly no one else could understand.

Sita immediately took Cadecus aside and quietly explained the situation to him, believing he was unaware of the details of their strange encounter. "That old woman has put a curse on the village, so that it rains, all day every day. Because of the constant storms, the villagers are completely dependent on the outside world for their survival. Everything they need that requires sunlight must be carried over the mountains. Even though the villagers despise this terrible place, they are also afraid to leave it. The village is surrounded by mountains, deserts, and even an ocean. Anyone who attempted to leave has never been heard from again."

"Are you saying this town has never seen the sun?" Cadecus asked sounding surprised.

"Almost never," Sita replied. "There is barely enough sunlight for them to survive. The old hag has cursed this village infecting it with fear and despair. The villagers despise the old witch, but are also afraid of her. So, the crisis has continued for many years. As a consequence, everything the people do is designed to endure the weather and avoid the witch. The people are weary after all this time, and they need relief."

"So what are you planning to do?" Cadecus asked curiously.

"I must do away with the dreaded old woman and save the village from their fate," Sita continued. "Remember Cadecus, you specifically told me to pick a difficult confrontation."

"I see," Cadecus replied with seemingly more uncertainty now. "So, what will you do?"

"The old woman has a magic book of spells that she hides behind her fireplace mantel that she uses to create the rain. I'm going to sneak into her shack and steal the book. Then I'm going to learn the spells, and rescue the village."

"So you haven't memorized the words to the specific incantations yet?" Cadecus wanted to know.

"No," Sita replied almost condescendingly. "It wouldn't be any challenge at all if I had already studied the actual spells ahead of time."

Cadecus's intuition showed him the girl was convinced of her ability, so didn't discuss the spell book any longer. He did, however, ask about the witch herself. "What will you do with the old woman?"

Sita smiled knowingly as if she had just outsmarted her mentor and guide. "That will be your job," she said definitively. "You must subdue the old woman, so I can steal the secret book."

Of course, the Thought Healer already knew Sita's plot, nevertheless, it provided a real test of her compassion. Would she actually want him to vanquish the old woman completely and end her life, or would she desire to spare her? Would Sita be able to stop the rain by learning and chanting the correct spells?

Cadecus decided to follow rather than lead. "When do you want me to subdue the old woman?" The Thought Healer asked. "And how do you want me to accomplish it?

"We will approach her shack this afternoon while there is at least a little daylight," Sita replied with a more commanding voice. "Take care of her in whatever way you think will be the most persuasive."

"No," Cadecus replied assertively. "I will not."

"Why not?" Sita blurted out, suddenly feeling nervous and less self-assured.

"Find out for yourself," Cadecus replied dryly

Sita quickly recovered her sense of humility and poise while responding to the Thought Healer's tone. "Something is wrong. Cadecus, what mistake am I making? You promised to help me."

The Thought Healer paused a moment and then explained, "I will distract the old woman long enough for you to steal the spell book, but that is all. I will not kidnap her, nor will I do away with her as you seem to suggest."

"Thank you, Cadecus," the girl exclaimed in relief. "You're right. I overreacted when I made plans to restrain the old woman. It won't happen again. Now, I'm ready."

After their somewhat strained discussion was over, the two sojourners hiked toward the old woman's hovel, far from the village, near the mountain foothills. When they arrived, they easily discerned an old dilapidated cottage with holes in the roof and cracks in the walls, making it appear uninhabitable. As they spied on the shack from a discreet distance, it wasn't long before Cadecus could see the old woman walking around inside the primitive dwelling. They approached closer. Then the Thought Healer kept his promise by luring the old woman outside by making peculiar animal sounds.

When the old woman finally vacated the shack, Sita immediately dashed inside, grabbing the spell book from its hiding place behind the mantel. She escaped outside through the back door feeling empowered by her victory.

But then, completely unexpectedly, the old woman reappeared and began pursuing her as best as her frail body would permit. In her haste, the old witch tripped over a tree root and tumbled head long on the ground. By the time Sita and Cadecus found the elderly woman and figured out what had happened, she seemed unconscious or worse.

Miraculously, the rain ceased. The storm clouds parted, the sun burst through an open sky. Sita smiled realizing that her story had a happy ending at last, despite the old woman's predicament at the end. The Thought Healer's unforeseen actions had altered her story somewhat, but now the rains had ended anyway. As can be imagined, the rest of the day was spent in celebration.

THE PROMISE OF LONG TERM RECOVERY

Sita strolled regally through the town, thoroughly reveling in the adulation of the wonderstruck villagers who were waving to her and gleefully dancing in the street. Before long, the bloated sewers and overflowing reservoirs rapidly drained out. The sun began to awaken the entire town and. For the first time in one hundred years, there was a sense of renewed hope and purpose.

However, even while the sun was still shining on the third day, the unimaginable happened. From deep within the earth, intense heat began to rise up through the still soggy ground igniting fires all over the village. Within hours, the entire town was covered with smoke so thick it was impossible for the citizens to escape. While the flames leapt from the ground to the buildings, every living inhabitant was at risk. Watching in horror, Sita finally realized the old woman's spell casting held back the violent heat and flames, before they could break through the water logged ground.

In a frenzied panic, Sita began searching through the spell book desperately searching for the right incantation that would bring back the rains. Her terror was so intense it nearly paralyzed her. All she could see were blurred words on indecipherable pag

The fires raged on. Soon the town was engulfed by the blaze. The panicked villagers fled toward the seashore or attempted escape through the mountain foothills. Sita was left with the spell book, alone and traumatized.

As the disaster spiraled downward into chaos, Cadecus wisely determined to end the story and release Sita from its horrible climax. Within the time it takes to awaken from a nightmare, they were both back at the village stream near Sita's house.

The fires were gone, but the horrific memory remained. Sita's sense of failure and shame became almost unbearable, as she attempted to explain herself to the Thought Healer. He stopped her abruptly. "That was the final test," Cadecus asserted impatiently. "If that story would have been real, you would have disrupted an entire world and endangered the lives of every living person in that defenseless village. Now the testing is over; prepare to leave home at dawn."

By now, Sita was completely devastated. No longer willing to follow Cadecus, she spoke her mind without reservation as the tears rolled down her cheeks. "No, Cadecus," she shouted out miserably. "I am no longer worthy to follow you. I consistently make costly mistakes that bring only misery to me and everybody else. You must know that by now. No matter how carefully I plan and no matter how thoughtfully I act, it never works out. Please leave me alone. I will not be persuaded to follow you ag

The Thought Healer, expecting this response from his student, was prepared to answer. "I made you fail." He replied candidly. "You were supposed to fail. In fact, I made certain that you would be defeated. It was I who cornered the old woman and brought the inferno. You were not meant to succeed."

Now, it was Sita who was truly angry. "What are you saying? Are you suggesting that you deliberately caused me to lose control of my own story?"

"Yes," Cadecus answered simply.

"Why would you do that?" she complained bitterly. "You always make me miserable, and all I feel is guilt and shame. Even with all my careful planning, I still fail terribly. Other than that I've learned nothing."

The Thought Healer listened patiently, then continued his explanation. "We learn little from success except pride and arrogance. However, from defeat we learn humility, patience, and compassion. I needed to teach you how to bear sorrow and defeat because soon we will be immersed in them.

The struggling world has a great need for our help at this time, and I needed to prepare you. The forces of darkness are in danger of crowding out the light. The time has come to shoulder the wheel of love and truth, so the way of darkness is expelled from the villages and pushed back into the jungle.

The world is staggering under the weight of poverty, injustice, and greed. It is stumbling toward the abyss in selfishness and despair. To succeed, we must be willing to bear defeat and disappointment until we are successful enough to remind the world of the inner sun within us all. Ultimately we cannot save the world from darkness entirely, but we can drive it back far enough, so the inner light will re-energize the world once more. No setback or defeat will vanquish us if we remember why we are here."

Sita, once again, was baffled by the Thought Healer's words. Even still, it did matter she was meant to lose control of her story. Since it was impossible to succeed, then, in fact, she hadn't really failed at all. This idea provided a little solace and reassurance, though her nerves were still badly f

"Tomorrow," Cadecus went on. "We begin our journey in earnest. We will sojourn to the Gonald River above the Enila Falls, and then trek high into the Dhala Mountains. In these secret and remote expanses, we will search for my friends. After locating these allies, we will attempt to capture and hold the notorious fortress city of Graganite which rules over the region beyond the Dhala Mountains."

Sita was stunned by the Thought Healer's statement. "Are you going to overthrow the Kingdom of Sutin?"

Cadecus answered simply and directly. "Sutin's father was a kind and generous king, but his son has become ruthless and ambitious. He has begun a campaign to outlaw civil liberties even as he taxes the poor who are dying of starvation. The population will soon be decimated if we don't intervene. The darkness has taken hold there, at Sutin's castle. We must terminate his reign of brutality and indifference before all hope is extinguished.

Sita now understood more fully the reasons for her harsh initiation and training. She suspected Cadecus knew the mission would be extraordinarily difficult. She recognized his toughness with her as a way of teaching self-discipline and meaningful service. Nevertheless, she was still uncertain whether she was willing to follow the Thought Healer, especially since she still doubted her own abilities. "Cadecus, I don't think I can do this," she said sadly.

This timid assertion did not resonate well with Cadecus who was unwilling to mollycoddle his wavering student. His mood became harsh and un-reassuring. "Child," he began, "It's time to make a decision. I've answered your many complaints and addressed your every insecurity. There's no more time to waste on your doubts and fears. The starving people of Sutin are in despair. Their terrible cries echo down the mountains and over the rolling meadows. It's time to begin. We must advance quickly now, so there is no time to say goodbye to your family and friends. If we succeed, you will meet up with them again. If we don't, they will have been conquered, and we will be dead."

The Thought Healer's statements were brutally candid to the point of cruelty. He had presented Sita with many ideas and emotions she couldn't possibly understand in such a short time. Nevertheless, she believed at least some of the strange things he had related to her. Sita understood she really had no choices at all. If Cadecus was right, her village would soon be attacked. She wasn't willing to allow invaders to destroy her town if she could prevent it

A part of her still didn't trust Cadecus. He had consistently led her to believe an event would occur, then something else entirely would unfold. She almost always believed in him because of her inner vision and his command over every situation. Yet she doubted his veracity at times, filling her with doubt and uneasiness

Overall, Sita was inclined to believe Cadecus was someone extraordinary despite her concerns about his trickery. She somehow could dimly see that the world could indeed be threatened by some evil; if only because Cadecus himself had the power to draw upon forces to confront it. This power included his ability to control events by creating frightening plot alterations in her stories. It was apparent that her mother, father, and brothers could soon be in mortal danger as well. There might be no other way to help rescue them if she left the Thought Healer's side now.

7. Cadecus Finds an Ally

By nightfall, Cadecus and Sita had journeyed many miles upstream where the Sequoia forests of Antolay dominated the landscape. Cadecus knew precisely where he was heading, despite the long, deep shadow of twilight. He advanced up the stream easily. Sita, however, was far more tentative. She followed Cadecus so closely, she sometimes bumped up against his heels. She scurried behind him nervously, listening to all the strange and haunting sounds of the Antolay forest. Her heart raced whenever she heard a rustling tree branch or sudden splash from the stream. At times even Cadecus hesitated briefly, listening intently to the mysterious woodland sounds. Finally, when the darkness had enveloped the surrounding wood, the distant moon was their only lamp.

Before long, Sita was exhausted and lagging behind. Cadecus didn't seem to notice her condition. At last, he uttered the words she so desperately yearned to hear. "Hurry up. We're nearly there."

This assurance of impending success bolstered the girl's spirits. She quickly caught up to her teacher. They arrived at a small clearing surrounded by gigantic Sequoia trees and dense vegetation. Cadecus paused a moment to make certain the location was correct. Then he called up to the tree canopy, limbs and creepers. Within a few minutes, a huge being swooped down from the trees, gliding to the ground.

"Cadecus!" the flying being exclaimed. "At last, you've come!"

"Yes, Deudal, we meet again, my friend," Cadecus replied warmly.

Sita was spellbound as she stared at the giant flying creature. He had the face of a mortal but the body of a colossal bird. His appearance was brown, like the surrounding forest. His wings were dark green and majestic. His very presence bespoke nobility and power.

Witnessing Sita's surprise, Cadecus introduced her to his friend. "This is Deudal," Cadecus began. "He is the last of the Treeganaut race. Deudal has agreed to help us in our approaching battle with Sutin".

"Yes," Deudal agreed. "Sutin and his armies entered our Antolay Forests many years ago and enslaved my entire nation. I haven't seen any of them in a very long time. I fear they are dead - murdered for their mystic talons".

"I don't understand," Sita inquired as politely as she could. "Why did Sutin wish to murder your friends to seize their claws?"

Cadecus tried to interrupt the inquisitive girl, but Deudal waved him aside and continued. "Our talons are not simply appendages like those of other birds. They are filled with a glowing blue liquid which has miraculous curative powers. If someone is fatally ill or wounded, the blue fluid will revive him."

Sita thought for a moment and then pressed on. "Mr. Deudal, is it possible someone could live longer if they saved enough blue liquid?"

"Perhaps," the birdman responded. "It is my belief that Sutin intends to steal all the blue liquid of my people, so he can stay alive for an indefinite period of time".

"Is that possible?" Sita replied in disbelief.

"It is," Deudal answered. "Sutin will become more reckless and more powerful if he continues to ingest the mystic substance. He can also use it to revive prisoners he wishes to interrogate or to employ it as a reward for those who risk their lives for him".

"Then he really is wicked!" Sita reacted in horror. "So, how are we going to stop him?"

"My people treasure the glowing blue essence, and we will not surrender it even if we're captured and tortured," Deudal answered solemnly.

Suddenly Sita realized intuitively what Deudal and Cadecus already knew. "You're immortal, aren't you?"

"You're right, Thought Healer," Deudal said, turning to Cadecus. "This child is intelligent."

Sita's rush of self-confidence and pride was apparent until Cadecus answered dryly, "Sometimes she is."

Not withstanding the Thought Healer's remark, some of Sita's excitement remained. She persisted in questioning the Treeganaut. "If your people are immortal, aren't they protected from Sutin's warriors?"

"Unfortunately not," Deudal replied gravely. "There is a way to end even an immortal's life."

Sita was so curious now that she couldn't stop herself. "And what is that?"

"If I reveal the secret to you," the birdman answered, "you'll know, and you'll tell".

8. An Alliance Is Forged

It was clear from Deudal's ominous remarks there was some significant reason he didn't choose to answer Sita's intrusive question. Respecting his wish to deflect her curiosity with an ambiguous reply, she decided to let the matter drop, at least, for now.

Cadecus and Deudal were becoming more serious as the evening progressed. Cadecus built a modest campfire; Deudal gathered fruits and tubers. Soon they were discussing plans for the days ahead. Sita, although sore and weary, listened intently.

"We must journey to Riverwood by tomorrow evening," the birdman asserted. "We need to find our companion, Atmun, before he advances into the Dhala Mountains. If we don't, he may attempt to conquer the Sutin Empire himself, and he will most certainly fail

"Riverwood is nearly thirty miles from here," Cadecus pointedly observed. "The child will never be able to walk that far!"

The word "child" was beginning to annoy Sita, especially since she felt she had already learned and experienced so much. Yet, she also agreed that thirty miles would be an almost impossible distance for her to trek in a single day. How could she possibly hike a full day and night with little chance to rest? Sita wanted to speak up and sound brave, but she knew from experience that exaggerating her abilities had often gotten her into trouble, so she kept silent.

Just when a feeling of dejection had begun to settle in on the group, Deudal let out a hearty laugh. Turning to Cadecus, he said, "Have you forgotten, Thought Healer; I can fly!"

Before Cadecus could reply, the birdman suddenly grabbed Sita by her backpack and swept her up into the clear blue sky. As Deudal flew ever higher, Sita gradually overcame her initial terror, quickly becoming familiar with Deudal's movements, as he glided and spiraled through the air. By the time they landed, everyone understood the meaning of Deudal's demonstration. The gigantic birdman could easily carry Sita above the treetops whenever she grew weary. It seemed like a perfect solution for Sita's inability to walk such a distance.

With a renewed sense of hope, the three companions rapidly advanced upstream. When Sita was too tired to continue, Deudal swept her up, setting her down further up the trail. Then they would both wait for Cadecus to rendezvous with them. As they lingered on the path, Sita asked Deudal questions about the mission. She especially wanted to know about Atmun. "Will Atmun be able to help us?" Sita asked quietly.

Deudal was slow to speak, but when he did, it was with an air of humility and respect. "Atmun is the wisest and possibly the oldest being in the entire kingdom. He has survived in the foothills of the Dhala Mountains for many, many years. But he is also the saddest being in the realm as well".

"Why?" Sita interjected. "If he is so wise, why isn't he happy or at least healthy?"

"Because," Deudal replied more forcefully, "Atmun has been bewitched by a spell he cannot break. He has been cursed with the ability to assume any identity except that of his true self".

Sita was bewildered by Deudal's explanation. "Are you saying Atmun can change into any being he chooses except himself?"

"Yes," Deudal replied softly. "Atmun cannot discover his true identity except at his moment of death. This is the burden he must carry".

"How does he know that he will discover his identity even at his death?" Sita persisted.

"He doesn't know for sure," Deudal replied. "But that is his belief; otherwise, he would surely despair. If Atmun doesn't recognize his own true self, even at death, then how can he ever solve the mystery of life?"

Before they could finish their discussion, the Thought Healer came jogging up the path. Catching up to Sita and Deudal, he took a swig from his turtle shell canteen. They resumed their trek along the fast moving stream. By the time they reached Riverwood, it was Cadecus who was the most exhausted. He collapsed under a large tree branch overlooking the rustic town. He took a number of deep cleansing breaths. After resting for several minutes, he had recovered enough strength to rise to his feet. He scanned the village cottages for some time until he spotted a specific dwelling. He pointed to the small hut at the far edge of Riverwood and exclaimed, "There is Atmun's house! Come, we must hurry!"

Even as they prepared to hike down the embankment and cross the meadow into the town below, Atmun appeared before them. He simply stepped out from behind a tall willow tree in front of them. The three travelers were shocked and silent at first, but soon recovered their composure. "How did you find us?" Cadecus asked with sense of humor and camaraderie in his voice.

Atmun began to laugh as well, "Your birdman friend was continually popping up over the trees. A child could have followed him."

Deudal became more serious while he considered the implications of Atmun's seemingly lighthearted remark. If Atmun had seen him flying over the treetops, maybe Sutin's scouts saw him as well. He smiled weakly at his wise old friend, but the three companions silently realized they might encounter the enemy soon.

Sita was unaware of any immediate danger. She focused on Atmun's strange appearance. He was indeed old with misshapen limbs and a gravelly voice. He also seemed nervous and weak. When Atmun noticed Sita and her critical glance, he instantly transformed himself into a dashing young knight. He said sarcastically, "Do you prefer this image instead?"

She was startled and didn't know how to respond. She had no idea Atmun knew what she was thinking. Finally, she asked, "Did you read my mind?" she asked bashfully. "Can you read my thoughts?"

"Yes," Atmun answered with a grin. "At your impressionable age, the thoughts were written all over your face!"

The three adults laughed uproariously at Sita's naïve comment. She blushed. At the moment, she was defenseless, feeling more vulnerable than ever. Luckily, Cadecus redirected the conversation in a more sober direction before Sita was completely humiliated.

"We still need one more ally," the Thought Healer interjected. "We cannot hope to defeat Sutin at Graganite without at least one more companion. We need Minerva"

"Yes," Deudal nodded in agreement. "The great enchantress from the high Dhala Mountains will certainly help us if she knows what we're planning".

Atmun was in immediate agreement. "Yes, Minerva will come. She vehemently opposes the reign of Sutin as much as any of us".

Sita, listening intently, became more intrigued as the discussion expanded. "Who is Minerva and why is she so important?"

Cadecus explained about the mystic conjurer. "Minerva is the most brilliant occultist in the entire world. She has the ability to create visions by altering perceptions of the past, present, and future. She can find and follow any kind of trail regardless of the circumstances. Her most miraculous power is her ability to exist simultaneously in two different places at once."

Deudal listening respectfully to Cadecus, agreed, "Having Minerva with us is the perfect choice for the last member of our team".

"I agree as well," Atmun interjected again, endorsing the notion.

It seemed that once again that Sita was in the metaphorical dark. "How can we five defeat an entire army?" she complained bitterly.

Her remark was quickly challenged by Cadecus. "We are trying to avoid an all out war, because it would create misery and death for scores of innocent people. In the chaos of conflict, even your brothers may be required to fight for your village's survival."

Deudal interrupted, attempting to help the young teen understand the Thought Healer's words in a less abrasive manner. "Sita," he said kindly. "We will have an army of our own. I will be our air corps; Cadecus will be our infantry and Atmun will be our scout. When we locate Minerva, we will be our artillery battery.

The world is not as it seems right now. Sutin and his hoard are extremely dangerous. They think and move with pride, greed, and savagery, so their actions will be somewhat predictable. Even their cruelty and cunning has a certain logic and underlying pattern. We will also have the elements of uncertainty and surprise as important capabilities."

It was obvious to young Sita that these beings she called friends were probably capable of magnificent feats of courage and strength. She still had no idea how she herself could possibly fit into this highly gifted group. She knew there would be something she that would be required to accomplish. The three tests of initiation administered by Cadecus were proof enough of that. But she still didn't understand what her real duties. This uncertainty, together with her past failures made the likelihood of her success seem remote.

With only one member of the team to locate, the growing expeditionary force approached the trail head at the foothills of the Dhala Mountains. Their jovial manner continued to help them forward. Sita drew strength from their calm sense of self-assurance. As the trail grew steeper and wound around the side of the mountains, the ascent became more treacherous. The group climbed relentlessly higher as the sunlight grew faint.

To her credit, Sita refused to be treated like a weakling and did her best to keep pace with the others. She didn't cry out or complain even when she caught her boot on a rock and nearly stumbled off the side of the mountain.

Nevertheless, Cadecus recognizing Sita's unspoken distress abruptly demanded that they all stop to rest periodically without mentioning the reason. Sita knew the truth and was grateful.

It was at one of these rest intervals on the mountain that they discovered Minerva, the very being they were seeking. Standing on an outcropping of rock high above them, she spoke in a booming voice they recognized instantly.

"Why do you search for me?" she demanded harshly.

"But you already know," Atmun shouted back.

The great mystic enchantress stood motionless on the rocks for several moments, obviously reading the thoughts of all the mountaineers. She rose higher in the sky and shouted, "Meet me at Emerald Lake near the summit. Be there tomorrow at sunset, or you won't meet me at all!"

The mysterious specter vanished as suddenly as she had appeared. The group of companions were left to explain Minerva's motives on their own. Cadecus was less inclined to question the mystic's warning than the others; he took the lead farther up the mountain trail. The others followed, maintaining their faith in the Thought Healer's intuition; but their doubts about Minerva's ultimatum was unsettling to them.

Unfortunately, even the weather seemed to conspire against them, as they slowly persevered with their ascent. The freezing wind and stinging snow grew so harsh that even Deudal was not immune to its ferocity. In a moment of uncharacteristic weakness, he nearly surrendered to the blizzard. At last, he cried out, "This wind is so dangerous, it's freezing my wings. They're so heavy I can barely keep them from dragging in the snow."

Sita, who was right behind him, was also badly frightened and completely exhausted. In fact, the entire group was in trouble. They faced a life or death decision. They either needed to descend the Dhala

Mountain trail immediately, or seek nearby shelter before the darkness left them completely exposed.

The howling wind swirling around them, they shouted to each other in an attempt to devise a plan. Their situation was rapidly deteriorating and with no natural shelters in view, they decided to retreat down the mountain. By the time they were halfway down, their bodies were numb and their nerves were strained.

The group was exhausted and disappointed when they finally reached a resting space after their dangerous descent. They felt betrayed by Minerva. Yet it seemed an impossible judgement to make based on their enduring friendship with her. At last, Deudal spoke the words that the rest of the group was thinking. "Why would Minerva give us a task that was impossible to accomplish? Why would she appear so cruel?"

It was at that precise moment that Sita provided her first truly helpful insight. "Maybe Minerva knows of some danger at Emerald Lake, and she was acting harshly in order to discourage us. Has Minerva ever spoken to you so angrily before?"

"No, never," Atmun answered quickly. "She has always been kind, loving, and even mischievous. It could be she is attempting to protect us by creating a challenge beyond our capabilities. Sita has made an important point. I wonder if Minerva had more than one audience when she was shouting down at us?"

Cadecus who now saw the merit of the other group members' arguments added his own question, "If Minerva is protecting us, who is protecting her?"

"And who is lurking in the shadows up there at the lake". Atmun interjected with an ominous tone.

It soon became obvious the group had probably solved one mystery only to be faced with another. They all sat in silence at the campfire near the base of the mountain, keeping their thoughts and fears to themselves. They all knew the identity of the lurking shadows at Emerald Lake; but no one wished to discuss their suspicions openly.

At last, Deudal brought up the subject in specific terms. "We must assume that Minerva is in some desperate trouble. Why else would she act the way she did? I can't even imagine how painful it must have been for her to send us away. We must liberate her despite her attempt to deceive us! The Sutin emperor and his forces are responsible for Minerva's distress. I feel certain of it. We need a strategy. We must discover a way to reach Emerald Lake undetected and then find out if our companion is safe."

9. The Search for Minerva

While Cadecus and the others were discussing ways to summit Mount Dhala, Minerva was being held captive by a platoon of Sutin infantry. The leader of the group, a muscular fiend, treated her cruelly and attempted to intimidate her, so she would reveal some secret he might find useful. Fortunately, however, the dim witted officer had no notion of Minerva's true identity or capabilities. Unknown to any of Sutin's soldiers, Minerva had been employing one her gifts periodically, so that she was sometimes in two places at the same time. This movement through inner space had allowed her to warn her friends on the mountain in a way that Cadecus and the others would secretly question. Minerva's harsh words and demeanor were also meant to frighten away anyone else who might be listening. Minerva had no idea that it was Sita who first understand her message.

Minerva was also aware that if she sent out a signal for help, her friends would rush up the mountain to save her regardless of the consequences. This would prove disastrous. The Sutin warriors would have been merciless to her friends if they were captured. Even Sita would not be spared. So, Minerva waited patiently, hoping her friends would have time to craft a viable strategy.

Near the base of Mount Dhala, Cadecus was describing an amazingly simple strategy that was shrewd enough to offer the possibility of success. When he began to describe it, his faith in himself and his idea inspired the others.

"We have climbed this mountain once," he began slowly, "but a storm stopped us before we could reach the summit. Tomorrow we will try again; but this time we'll form two independent teams. Atmun and I will ascend as we did yesterday. If a storm overtakes us, we'll return to the safest point we were able to reach on our last climb. Deudal and Sita will fly as high and as far up the mountain as possible. If the cold begins to freeze your wings, Deudal, you and Sita must land on the mountainside and build a fire intense enough to melt the ice from them. I have gathered a bundle of hardwood logs. I will give Sita a powerful flint stone. If Atmun and I are fortunate enough to avoid any storms, we will all meet together near Emerald Lake. Remember to stay away from the lake itself until we are all together near the northern shore. Are there any questions?"

The Thought Healer's plan was so surprising that it required the others to consider it for a while before they could even respond. At last, Atmun asked the most obvious question. "Isn't this plan really dangerous, especially for Sita?"

Before Sita could answer, Cadecus quickly replied. "Sita has been well prepared. She is intelligent and resourceful. Besides, it hardly seems fair to leave Minerva to her fate when she has just warned and protected us. Sita, what would do you think?"

"I'm not afraid," the girl answered in a calm and reassuring tone. "Cadecus is right. He has shown me many things, now I must help. I won't leave your friend Minerva to die if I can do anything to prevent it. I won't leave her especially after she has risked her safety not even knowing if we could rescue her. She doesn't know me, yet she thought of my welfare over her own."

"Then it's settled," Cadecus responded assertively. "We leave at dawn".

Meanwhile, high in the mountains at Emerald Lake, Minerva glimpsed the Thought Healer's plan. Her intuition and logical reasoning led her to the insight that her friends would soon attempt to deliver her from her Sutin captors. She also realized that their attempt to free her had unforeseen difficulties which only she could truly comprehend. As she awaited their arrival, Minerva began to formulate her own strategy to assist them when they arrived. If she could only distract the unimaginative Sutin warriors long enough, she could assist them with her rescue.

THE PROMISE OF LONG TERM RECOVERY

As Minerva waited patiently for her comrades to arrive, Cadecus and his comrades were already ascending toward Emerald Lake. Deudal positioned the firewood in Sita's pack and hoisted her on his shoulders. Soon they were soaring up the mountainside hoping to avoid detection. At the same time, Atmun and Cadecus began scrambling up the mountain trail as swiftly as their bodies and the terrain would allow. By the late afternoon, Deudal and Sita were approaching the summit., Cadecus and Atmun were still only halfway to the lake.

Despite their success up the mountain, both Sita and Deudal recognized the need for caution and patience. They built a crackling fire to keep from freezing. This gave Cadecus and Atmun more time to reach them, so they could act in unison to liberate Minerva.

It was nearly sundown by the time Cadecus and Atmun reached Sita and Deudal. Then, without warning, another storm blew down from the summit. Within a few hours, the fuel for the fire was spent, and the four would be liberators seemed in need of rescue themselves.

But their courage didn't fail them. Instead of retreating a second time, they continued their ascent with Deudal spreading his wings to partially block the impact of the howling wind and swirling snow. With Deudal in the lead, they finally reached the summit just as the Treeganaut's wings completely froze. He fell to the ground, concealing his agony with difficulty.

The team knew they needed to act quickly. It was painfully clear that if Deudal didn't warm up soon, he would die. With the Sutin camp close by, it was obvious the enemy warriors would probably be loitering around a life saving bonfire. The camp itself would be at least partially sheltered from the unforgiving storm. For Duedal to survive, he needed that fire.

Atmun, sensing Deudal's mortal danger, instantly transformed himself into a Sutin soldier and advanced directly into the enemy encampment. When the soldiers caught sight of him, they brandished their swords, waiting for Atmun to speak. "I have captured one of the

Treeganaut beasts, and I need help dragging him into camp," he called out.

Cadecus grasped Atmun's plan in an instant - pretending that Deudal was his prisoner, so he could lead him to the bonfire and save his life. He motioned for Sita to follow him. They both silently slipped behind a turn in the mountain trail, watching the scene unfold from their secret vantage point.

Amazingly, Atmun's transformation into a Sutin soldier totally deceived the enemy warriors. One soldier raced up to Deudal and helped the disguised Atmun drag the birdman over to their blazing fire. While Deudal was slowly regaining his senses, Atmun carefully scanned the camp to discover all he could. He identified twelve soldiers which were many more than they had expected. There was no sign of Minerva who was the only reason he and his companions had ascended the mountain. In an effort to learn more about her whereabouts, Atmun tried to engage the soldiers in conversation. "I thought I'd be alone up here on my mission. What brings all of you up here?"

The soldiers seemed surprised by Atmun's question, and instead of answering, they became more aggressive. "We are all on this mountain for the same reason. Why don't you know?"

Atmun could feel himself losing his advantage and tried to recover. "Well, one thing is certain. I'm here to drag the Treeganaut right into your lap!"

This cunning remark saved Atmun and protected the rescue mission. Not only did it seemingly prove his allegiance, but it also cleverly deflected the soldier's threatening attitude. Even more importantly, Atmun's bravado also enticed one of the other soldiers to boast about Minerva. "You might have seized a birdman; but we have taken Minerva the witch, prisoner. That was why Emperor Sutin stationed us here in the first place. You just got lucky."

Despite the soldier's claim, Atmun still couldn't locate Minerva anywhere in the camp. He decided to press the soldiers for a more detailed response. "You couldn't capture the mystic witch! She's too clever for any of you!"

Right on cue, the officer in charge shouted haughtily, "Look behind that rock and you can see for yourself."

Atmun casually strolled behind the boulder the soldier had pointed out. He saw nothing but more rock formations. Then he stared down on the ground and observed a huge chasm at least twenty feet deep. There at the bottom, chained, gagged, and blindfolded lay Minerva seemingly unconscious or dead.

It was nearly impossible for Atmun to conceal the sorrow and anger overwhelming his heart. In an almost uncontrollable moment of rage, he was tempted to attack all twelve soldiers on his own. But he quickly realized his anger might very easily get his companions killed. So instead, he asked the soldiers more about their captive.

"I can't believe you captured her," Atmun began, attempting to sound impressed and surprised.

"Yes," the Sutin leader asserted proudly. "The arrest of the old hag will greatly please the emperor. He has long suspected that she is a threat to him and his kingdom. The truth is she frightens him because of her ability to cast treasonous spells. Now that we have both captured Minerva and the Treeganaut, we will be rewarded for bringing them to the emperor's city of Graganite. Now, retrieve the birdman and toss him into the pit. We'll break camp at first light tomorrow."

"Excuse me," Atmun spoke out, still disguised. "Shouldn't we finish thawing out the Treeganaut before we dump him in the cavern? Sutin himself may want to interrogate him before he severs his talons."

"Of course," the Sutin officer replied defensively. "That's what I meant. Finish thawing him out, and then dump him."

As Atmun positioned Deudal closer to the blazing fire to fully restore his wings, Cadecus and Sita were aware that the crisis could worsen at any moment. The Thought Healer knew that Atmun could not deceive the soldiers for long, because he was so concerned about

Minerva and Deudal that he might act impulsively. He eventually might attempt to confront the soldiers by again altering his appearance. This could further endanger their companions and could even bring about their deaths.

Before long, the time for specific action had come. Cadecus, in a moment of spontaneity brought on by his concern, revealed his location by stepping directly into the enemy camp. He left Sita unprepared and frightened, as she waited behind in her hiding place. "Hello," Cadecus said cordially to the first soldier he encountered. "I wish to speak to the officer in charge."

The soldier didn't respond to the Thought Healer's friendly tone." I'm in charge!" he bellowed. "Who are you?"

"I, sir, am Emperor Sutin's health minister," Cadecus shot back more assertively. "I have been sent to quarantine all soldiers on this mountain who have been exposed to the plague."

The haughty officer now became less belligerent and condescending. "Are you suggesting the plague has broken loose again, Mr. Health Minister?"

"Yes, I am. The emperor is concerned the contagion will spread throughout his kingdom. I must examine all of you for fever, dizziness, and nodules."

"None of us is infected," the officer insisted. "I would have certainly discovered it myself."

"You are not a physician!" Cadecus responded forcefully, realizing that his ruse was seemingly effective. "Shall I tell Emperor Sutin that you are more qualified at diagnosing the plague than his chief health minister?"

The very suggestion that Sutin might be displeased clearly frightened the conceited officer. He quickly amended his remarks. "I meant no disrespect. I just think I would have known if any of my warriors were ill. But go ahead and examine them."

"Don't you mean *the emperor's soldiers*?" Cadecus asked pointedly.

"Yes, of course. The emperor's soldiers," the officer quickly replied sheepishly.

With no further argument, the Sutin leader ordered his men to be examined by the kingdom's would be physician. Atmun, who had been tending to Deudal, hid himself, waiting for Cadecus to reveal his real intentions. After all twelve soldiers were scrutinized, the Thought Healer declared the camp was free of disease. Cadecus then called out to Sita. "Come, my child. The camp is safe."

Immediately, Sita wandered into the warriors' camp like a phantom. She quickly found Cadecus and said, "Thank goodness grandfather. I was worried."

Before the Sutin leader could complain, Cadecus cut him off. "This is my granddaughter, Sita. She is the emperor's youngest food taster. Emperor Sutin wishes her to gather fruits and vegetables from every camp to determine if they are safe for him to eat. Now feed her. She has no ill will toward any of you. She only wishes to serve the emperor."

The Sutin soldiers did as they were ordered, but they certainly couldn't have anticipated what happened next. From behind the camp, Atmun left his secluded hiding place and stood before the soldiers at the campfire. He appeared very ill and exhibited all the symptoms of the deadly Crimson Plague. He was sweating profusely, shaking as if he were about to fall down, under his chin and arms were dark boil-like nodules.

Cadecus acted as if he were outraged. "Why did you hide this soldier from me? This is treason!"

The officer was so confused, he could hardly speak. "He just wandered into camp yesterday!" he wailed. "He hasn't even been around us!"

Atmun, understanding his companion's entire plan was working, immediately fell down on the snow covered ground and pretended to lose consciousness

The terror stricken soldiers were too frightened to respond. Cadecus ordered, "Throw that soldier down into the cave with Minerva!"

The officer in charge immediately picked up on the Thought Healer's mistake.

"How did you know about the old witch?" He demanded, regaining his control. Then he thought for a moment and said angrily, "It occurs to me that there seems to be a lot of coincidences happening all of sudden. First, the solitary soldier surprises us with a Treeganaut, then a physician and his granddaughter suddenly appear trying to convince us there is a plague loose on the mountain. Worst of all, you all claim to be emissaries of Sutin himself, and yet you haven't shown us any real proof."

As soon as his harangue was over, the officer ordered his soldiers to bind all four

spies. He had them under guard by the fire while he thought about what to do next.

He desperately needed to discover the truth about their identities and their purpose for infiltrating his camp. Clearly, they were lying about who they were; however, they still could be secret agents of the emperor. At last, his patience was spent, and he decided to rely on his own brutality that had often been so effective in his other interrogations. He turned to one of his soldiers and ordered, "Throw the girl in the pit. If we don't hear the truth about this plot by dawn, we'll poison the 'food taster' with hemlock."

Cadecus allowed the soldiers to push Sita down into the cave, partly because he knew she was strong enough to face her own fears, but mostly so she could assist Minerva. When he realized his student was relatively safe, for a while at least, he told the officer the truth about their mission. He mentioned Minerva and how they needed to forge an alliance to confront the emperor in a way that would persuade him to improve the lives of the inhabitants of his kingdom. By the time he was finished, Cadecus already understood the consequences.

"You're traitors!" The officer bellowed furiously. "You will be executed for your treachery, of that you can be certain!"

The brutal remarks of the Sutin leader were savage but understandable. It seemed obvious to the Thought Healer and all the other captives, they had overestimated their own abilities and intelligence. If they couldn't defeat only twelve soldiers, how could they expect to overcome an entire army? It was clear that even stealth had failed them. The mission seemed over before it had truly begun.

Yet, sometimes what seems real is an illusion. While Sita was attempting to assist Minerva by removing her shackles, she quickly discovered that Minerva's body felt virtually weightless. Indeed, it seemed to almost rise up and float likes a bubble through the air. Sita was naturally frightened and confused by Minerva's condition; but she also considered the situation to be a sign of hope

Sita was correct in her assumption. Minerva, who seemed frail and helpless, had actually been waiting for her friends to act. Now, certain that her comrades had done all they could, she suddenly flew out of the chasm and shot up high over the abyss. Hovering above the enemy camp, she created a terrifying spectacle of war, complete with booming cannon explosions, rifles volleys, and the horrifying screams of warriors in terror. While the soldiers attempted to remain calm, Minerva's "attack" intensified, and within a quarter of an hour, the soldiers were scurrying down the mountain like frightened children.

Cadecus and the others were also badly shaken until they understood the source of the chaos was Minerva's powerful magic. When she was sure the soldiers wouldn't return, the great enchantress untied the group and collected Sita from inside the frigid chasm.

They assembled by the fire. Atmun transformed into his more sage like persona. He asked Minerva the question that everyone wanted to ask. "Minerva," he began respectfully. "Why didn't you help us sooner? You knew we were in trouble."

"I needed to know what you were capable of accomplishing on your own," she replied simply. "Besides, I did help you by warning you."

"But Minerva," Deudal complained. "We only ascended to the lake in order to save you. Otherwise, we wouldn't have put ourselves in danger."

It was now Minerva's turn to scold. "Do you think Emperor Sutin has twelve soldiers guarding his fortress at Graganite? If you are so easily defeated by twelve soldiers, you will certainly fail when challenged by more. You needed to find this out for yourself through your own experience."

This clear assessment embarrassed them all, not because it was cruel, but because it was true. Cadecus, who actually made the biggest blunder by identifying Minerva's presence and location, was the most to blame. He said nothing and waited for Minerva to continue. When she did, the entire group now felt unexpectedly inspired.

"Listen to me," she said mysteriously. "It is impossible for us to defeat the armies of Sutin. That isn't why we are together on this mission. Everything we think, say, and do are possible sources of hope that may lighten the burdens of the citizens of Sutin's world. We must learn to walk forward by constantly falling down. Too much success, too early, brings out only selfishness and pride. But there is more. Tell them Thought Healer."

Cadecus sat silently for a long time. He began to explain a mystery so deep it was difficult for the others to believe or understand. "Some of you here understand more about me than you've revealed, but now the time has come for all of you to know. I am Cadecus, a resident of a distant kingdom beyond the sky called Haventry. I have been here for a thousand years seeking out individuals who may be worthy to join my fellow citizens on our home world. My mission is defined by my name – Thought Healer. My purpose is to help mortals overcome the thoughts and feelings that burden them with sorrow created by anger, greed, and pride. By creating an infinite number of possible scenarios, I make it possible for them to overcome their negative thoughts and beliefs, so they can live in harmony with themselves and the world around them. Over time, I can teach some to transcend thought entirely, first for minutes, then for days, and then, for a few, eternity. After sufficient experiences, thoughts are healed and overcome, making it possible for mortals to inhabit my world.”

Cadecus's frightening and bizarre account was too much for the group to totally grasp. They couldn't see how his remarks could be hopeful for them personally. It was nearly impossible for them to understand that life itself could appear to be a kind of drama created by Cadecus, simply to dredge up the groups’ weaknesses and failings.

Minerva was not surprised by the Thought Healer's deeply philosophical remarks. Her own testimony was equally shocking.

“I too am originally from Haventry. Cadecus and I have been stationed here on Htrae for a very long time. We have been searching for individuals of all races who seem to understand the significance of the ‘One behind the many’, those individuals who have a glimpse of a different way of being.”

“This compassionate attitude and intuitive propensity are greatly needed at this time in your world,” Minerva continued. “This planet of almost infinite capacity is slipping into darkness, a darkness that could prevail over the light for eons to come. Some, including Cadecus and I, and possibly all of you, must turn back the darkness, so the Light may once again shine through the gathering gloom and despair. Then, the Light will illuminate your world again, and all beings who call this Htrae planet their own will again know peace and stability. But the time is short, and the Light bearers are few. We must move quickly and decisively.”

Minerva's added explanation brought little comfort. Her words induced more fear than hope in their heart and minds. Nevertheless, they now felt more certain that Minerva and Cadecus were telling the truth, no matter how terrible it sounded. As they sat quietly around the fire, the various members began to think more deeply about the meaning of both Cadecus's and Minerva's enigmatic revelations. Before long, they all had questions about their own individual experiences with the two mystic beings.

Atmun spoke first. He desperately wanted information about his real identity. His questions, directed at Cadecus, were both direct and soulful. He gazed at the Thought Healer with a piercing stare and asked, "Is it possible you and Minerva both know my true identity?"

"Yes, it is true," Cadecus replied simply. "I have always known who you are."

"And you never told me?" Atmun asked with a trace of anger rising in his voice.

"You wouldn't have understood," the Thought Healer responded evenly. "You cannot be told. You must learn the truth yourself."

Finally becoming frustrated, Atmun shouted, "No more deceit! And no more clever words to avoid answering my questions. I want to know who I am, and I want to know now!"

"Very well," Minerva intervened. "I'll tell you the truth. You are nobody."

Atmun was puzzled and irritated by the mystic's strange response. "How can I be nobody?"

Now Cadecus interrupted. "Atmun, Minerva has given you the best answer you can understand at the moment. Clearly, you can transform into any mortal, and yet none of them are who you truly are. So, while you sojourn with us, you are 'nobody', at least for now."

These unintelligible replies to Atmun's desperate inquires were too much for the old man to bear. He began to weep. As he was sinking into the depths of despair, Sita approached him with a measure of comfort far beyond the capacity of most adolescents. "Atmun, we are all really nobody when you think about it. We don't know where we have come from, and in many ways, we don't understand where we are right now. It is all part of an illusion, a dream in which we are all somehow asleep. I believe the answers to all our questions lie before us on our journey even if we don't know where we will finish."

"The answers are also within you," Cadecus softly added. "Atmun, you must solve this riddle on your own. It would be helpful if we all considered ourselves to be 'nobody' because that is a kind of subtle identity of its own. Enough word play, the time has come for action. The fortress city of Graganite is only a few miles away below the next Dhala Mountain pass. We need to advance in that direction, devising a plan along the way. It is time to forget our own wants and needs for the good of your Htrae world."

The other team members, realizing their questions would now go unanswered, kept their doubts and suspicions to themselves. Their own personal histories would have to wait for a more auspicious time.

10. The Conflict of Good and Evil Commences

With Cadecus as commander and Minerva as counselor, the small band of revolutionaries traversed the mountain pass stopping only long enough to discover the narrow trail. Minerva's mystical tracking ability located short cuts and switch backs running along the steep and dangerous slopes, saving precious energy and time. Despite their impending confrontation, no one was able to formulate a proposal for their attack, or if they had, they weren't sharing it with the others.

Despite this inability to devise a plan, the group had traveled close enough to the fortress at Graganite to observe its defenses and the dilapidated village huddled beside it. Carefully studying the scene from their mountain hiding place, they could see a huge castle rising through the sky. They could also discern enemy soldiers stationed at every turret and more warriors keeping watch at the base of the fortress itself. Encircling the entire structure stretched a foul looking moat for one hundred yards in all directions. Beyond the moat, the poverty stricken villagers labored in the fields and tended their livestock. From their vantage point, Cadecus and the others espied Sutin sentinels terrorizing the farmers with wild gestures and strident commands. It wasn't long before the rebels on the ridge realized that their task was impossible.

They huddled together throughout the night, attempting to create an effective strategy. Just before dawn, Cadecus, yet again, pointed out the purpose of their mission. "Remember," he advised. "We don't need to defeat Sutin and his forces. We simply need to find a way to allow the light to expand."

"Then we must defeat Sutin, at least!" Deudal suddenly asserted forcefully. "He is responsible for the kidnapping of the entire Treeganaut race! He must die!"

"No," Minerva sharply replied. "We will not defeat evil with evil. Not here. Not now. You see the vast army Sutin commands. We can't challenge them all directly. We need something much more subtle. What we need is an illusion, a deception so powerful everyone in the fortress and the village will be terror stricken."

"Yes," Cadecus agreed. "We need to create an alternate portrayal of their Graganite world. We need a trick of the light."

"What do you mean exactly?" Atmun asked with immediate interest.

"Almost everyone accepts reality as it is presented to them," the Thought Healer continued. "What is the one thing that almost all beings are afraid to ponder?"

"Death," Deudal broke in. "Death is the one thing that terrifies almost all beings."

"Correct," Cadecus agreed. "So we must create the illusion that death is arriving. Now, how can we do that?"

The group members were silent for an excruciatingly long time; at last Sita came up with the perfect solution. "We could create the illusion that the world is ending. We could make everyone believe the world is going to be destroyed."

"Yes," Minerva answered for everyone. "Sita's idea offers the illusions of fear, instability, and judgment. If Sutin and his armies believe the world is ending, they may break ranks and scatter in confusion. Even Sutin himself will be terrified because he can't live for eternity, especially if there is no place for his eternity to exist!"

All five members were truly excited about Sita's idea. They all recognized an opportunity to employ their unique strengths and experiences against Sutin and his warriors.

With a glimmer of hope finally providing a sense of direction and purpose, the group of interlopers discussed their plans in more specific terms. Minerva, the most gifted of all the team members, began the discussion as if she were casting roles in a play.

"Atmun, you will be our fearless prophet who will convince the inhabitants of Graganite that the judgment day has come. Deudal, you will become the merciless dragon who punishes the wicked, and Sita you will be the orphan who persuades the citizenry that the prophet speaks the truth."

"And Minerva and I," Cadecus added enthusiastically, "will create phantoms, illusions, and feelings of dread that will take root within the minds of Sutin and his kingdom."

When Minerva and the Thought Healer had finished, there was a palpable sense of awkwardness among the group members. Despite Cadecus's and Minerva's overpowering self-confidence, the others were not so easily convinced. Remembering their many failures in the past, they weren't as eager to risk everything on a scheme which was so quickly conceived and alarmingly short on details. Even worse, when Sita and Deudal were about to discuss their concerns with Minerva and Cadecus, they observed that the two powerful out-worlders had vanished.

The three remaining team members, disappointed and more than a little frightened, knew it wasn't unusual for Minerva and Cadecus to set a plan in motion and then promptly disappear. Their disappearances were also not surprising because these tests of bravery and perseverance were meant for their own emotional growth and spiritual maturity. These present circumstances were different in intensity and importance. The drama about to be acted out, had a compelling sense of importance about it. This truth led all three group members to doubt themselves and question the judgment of their powerful friends.

"This is an impossible situation," Deudal complained bitterly. "How are we going to perform these tasks with no direction or assistance?"

"You're right," Atmun concurred. "We have no strategy to attack Sutin or his forces. It must mean that Minerva and Cadecus want us to remain here and wait for them to return."

"No," Sita said flatly. "This plan is meant to include all of us, even now. We all know Cadecus has disappeared before, often at crucial moments like this. In the past, I was certainly angered and confused by his lack of direction, but it's important for us to begin the deception now without waiting for more details."

Deudal and Atmun were both still cautious. But they dared not reveal their trepidation especially in front of such an extraordinary child. So, without further debate, they approached the village.

When the three actors drew near, they gathered their courage and hiked through the woods bordering the shabby Graganite town. Upon reaching the shacks nearest their position, they halted to plan their next move. However, just when their conversation was about to begin in earnest; Atmun unexpectedly raced into the village street, and began shouting out the obscure prophesies about the end of the world.

Minerva, sensing Atmun's movements, created her first illusion, using her magic to blot out the sun behind dark and ominous clouds. Atmun, recognizing and deeply appreciating Minerva's intervention, yelled out even louder: "Citizens of Graganite! Hear me well! The Day of Judgment approaches! The time to change your ways has come! Your world is doomed! The end has come at last! Turn from your wickedness while there is still time!"

Unfortunately, but predictably, Minerva's spectacle wasn't frightening enough to actually intimidate the arrogant soldiers. It only created a sense of terror in the villagers who immediately scooped up their children and fled into their hovels. Soon, only the Sutin warriors were still on the street. They were not amused. They deeply resented Atmun's sudden power over the town. Quickly surrounding the solitary figure and seizing him by the neck, they demanded, "Who are you?"

Atmun, whether in fear or inspiration, uttered the first words that entered his mind. "I am nobody."

The soldiers interpreted Atmun's statement as self-righteous and insulting. They threw him to the ground, binding his hands behind his back. When it became clear that Atmun wasn't going to be rescued, he cried out, "Minerva, Cadecus, help me!"

When there was no response to Atmun's call, the soldiers grabbed him by the arms, dragged him to his feet, and led the bewildered soothsayer toward the castle and Sutin's court.

Horrified, Sita and Deudal retreated into the shadows of the forest. It was now their turn to step into the scene. Deudal, remembering his role, covered his body and wings with bright vermilion ochre from a nearby stream bed and watched Sita cover her arms, face, and clothes with mud and leaves. When they were ready, the two actors entered the village and approached the remaining soldiers. Minerva continued her horrific spectacle, now adding lightning, thunder, and a driving rain to her spell. Sita, in a moment of courage shouted, "You have seized the prophet, but you can't ignore his message! The Day of Judgment is here! Surrender your weapons and repent! This ferocious dragon, you see beside me, is from the underworld, and soon he will strike, destroying the arrogant warriors of Sutin!"

At first, the soldiers were captivated by Sita's bravery and sincerity, but as the downpour persisted, Deudal's vermillion disguise and Sita's mud began to wash off. The soldiers grew more brazen and sarcastic as they closely observed Duedal and Sita's naïve disguises. Now, it was the soldiers' turn to threaten. "You're a meddlesome little witch and your horrifying dragon is just a disgraced Treeganaut who hid in the woods while his comrades were attacked and captured!"

"It seems like you're always hiding Treeganaut!" another soldier jeered mockingly. "Did the girl help you with your terrifying costume?"

The lead officer of the sentinels spoke up. "Take the birdman to the castle and let him join his clan!"

"What about the child?" another soldier inquired.

"Let her go," the officer ordered. "Maybe if we release her, she'll bring another birdman to us!"

The soldiers all enjoyed their superior's sarcastic barb. They immediately followed his order. After tethering Deudal to a coarse rope, they departed the village, leading the birdman. He felt defeated and alone, his only comfort knowing he remained by Sita's side even though he could have easily glided away. The Sutin officer sparing Sita gaving Deudal the sense that he was, at least partially responsible for her escape.

Atmun crossed the bridge over the squalid moat and entered the gigantic, intimidating Sutin fortress. Alone and despairing because of his own failure, and that Cadecus and Minerva had not rescued him. As the soldiers shoved him through the gate, bullying him down the stairs to his rat infested dungeon cell, he was so melancholy that even death seemed to be a better fate.

Despite Atmun's feelings of terror and gloom, he discovered that he wasn't alone. After the soldiers left, he regained control of his unreliable emotions and recognized Cadecus in the adjacent dungeon cell. In a shriek of excitement, he yelled, "Cadecus. Is that really you?"

"Lower your voice!" the Thought Healer whispered harshly. "If the guards find out we're friends, they are sure to separate us."

Atmun instantly lowered his voice, asking "How did you get here?"

Cadecus laughed softly replying, "I just strolled in through the front door, so to speak," Cadecus answered. "But how did you get here, Atmun? I thought you we're going to proclaim judgment day in the guise of a prophet

"I did," Atmun replied becoming dejected again. "But I was arrested after only a few minutes. So, I was no help at all."

"Don't be so sure," the Thought Healer reassured. "It was necessary for both of us to be captured. Your prophetic words were needed prompts so the soldiers would bring you before Sutin."

"I don't understand," Atmun replied in confusion. "How does getting captured further our mission?"

The Thought Healer smiled, saying, "Sutin is about to have a very bad nightmare, and you will be his tormenter."

"Do you really mean I was supposed to be locked up in this filthy cell?"

Yes," Cadecus replied. "But now we must prepare you for your audience with Sutin at his court. He will have his prophetic dream tonight, and you will be brought before him tomorrow. Sutin doesn't realize you are here yet. Tomorrow the guards will escort you to his throne to be tried for treason."

The Thought Healer's statement terrified his friend. "How will I defend myself when I appear before Sutin? What should I say?"

"What did you say to the soldiers in the village?" Cadecus inquired.

"I told them that I am nobody," Atmun answered feebly.

"Good. Very good," Cadecus exclaimed. "I want you to continue repeating that exact statement tonight and tomorrow. Do you understand what it means yet?"

"I am nobody suggests that every identity I assume will eventually fade away, so one specific transformation can never be permanent. The absence of these identities reveals the silent background on which my transformations occur. So, in essence nobody is the background behind 'everyone' and 'everything.'"

"Yes, yes," Cadecus concurred excitedly. "It's like taking a ball of yarn you have created by gathering different colored strands. When all the strands are removed, nothing is left. Likewise, even thoughts, or in your case, every physical transformation, is only an illusion you believe to be real."

"We accept reality as it is presented to us," Atmun emphatically replied, remembering the Thought Healer's earlier words. "How do we use this knowledge to our advantage?"

"We must create an illusion for Sutin and his court to witness," Cadecus answered mysteriously. "It is important you don't change form, no matter what happens. You must continue to identify yourself in the same manner as you have been."

"Do you mean I should continue to say that 'I am nobody'?" Atmun asked pointedly.

"Yes," Cadecus solemnly replied. "But you must also do something else. I want you to observe everything without trying to interpret it."

"I'm lost," Atmun said with a look of uncertainty. "What do you mean?"

"It means you must see everything 'as it is' without adding your own thoughts and impressions to it. In other words keep your mind open."

"I still don't understand," Atmun answered, more confused than ever.

"Look at these iron bars and tell me what you see", the Thought Healer instructed.

"I see iron bars keeping us prisoner. I can't bend the bars and I will probably never see the outside world of Htrae again," Atmun mused, drifting back into despair.

The Thought Healer smiled knowingly and replied, "All you really see are the iron bars. Everything else are your own thoughts, fears, and imagination."

Atmun remained skeptical, "How will keeping an open mind help us?

"Soon, Minerva and I will create more strange illusions and dreams that are meant to affect the citizenry of Graganite," Cadecus whispered. "You must discern that these deceptions are unreal so you don't panic. Then you won't do anything impulsive like the inhabitants will. Now, practice the awareness of nothingness. You will need this skill by tomorrow. Try to rest."

Atmun followed the Thought Healer's instructions, but felt uncertain and vulnerable regarding the great teacher's guidance. No matter how he focused his mind, it remained restless and anxious, causing him to lose his equanimity.

Deudal's plight was much more troubling than the circumstances of either Atmun or Cadecus.

The birdman was a valuable trophy for the Sutin emperor. He paraded Deudal through the castle like a sacred relic. By the time he reached the foul smelling dungeon, he had seen his Treeganaut comrades stuffed as wall sculptures or dismembered for jewelry. The awful brutality of it all left Deudal outraged and nauseous. When he was thrown into his cell, he was consumed by rage and despair. Atmun and Cadecus were exceedingly careful not to reveal themselves until the guards were gone.

Atmun spoke first. "Deudal, Cadecus and I are here. Don't be afraid."

"I'm not afraid!" Deudal shot back. "I'm angry!"

Cadecus again cautioned his friends to lower their voices. He remarked, "It is almost dawn. The time for our deliverance is almost here. Soon the guards will come to escort us to Sutin. Be ready."

As Cadecus was counseling his fellow prisoners, Sita was abandoned, wandering alone in the forest. She couldn't comprehend all that had occurred, but was still willing to persevere, if only she knew what to do. After several hours aimlessly searching for any useful trail or clue, she suddenly happened upon Minerva, the great conjurer herself.

"Don't be afraid, child," Minerva declared. "You and I will do our part to save the villagers and rescue our friends."

Sita was glad to see Minerva, but was less convinced about the mystic's optimism.

"We have been easily defeated every time we've faced the enemy," she pointed out. "In fact, you can't even call them defeats. We have been surrendered without a fight and let the Sutin soldiers arrest us. What kind of plan is that?"

"A good plan," Minerva replied, ignoring Sita's tone. "Now the trap is set."

Sita saw their circumstances very differently. "Yeah, we're the ones who are trapped!"

THE PROMISE OF LONG TERM RECOVERY

Before Sita could continue expressing her frustrations, Minerva was striding down the cobblestone road that led directly to the Graganite Castle. Fearing she would be left behind again, Sita ran to catch up. Trekking down the royal road, approaching the castle moat, not a single soldier attempted to detain them. At first, Sita assumed that the soldiers didn't consider them to be a threat, and so ignored them. However, when Minerva jumped on to the drawbridge, Sita realized they were invisible and free to advance at will.

Freely moving through the opulent palace chambers through the cold ivory halls, they found the emperor's throne room. Upon entering Minerva paused, awaiting the evil despot's appearance. Sita, completely mystified by Minerva's movements, remained courageous and silent, despite her anxiety. She dared not even imagine what her powerful friend was doing; but she was also afraid to leave her side.

Sita never could have predicted the events that unfolded before her as the dawn illuminated the castle. Sutin had anxiously entered the chamber, all his petty advisors humbly following. As he traversed the room, it became very clear that something was terribly wrong. Sutin's appearance was wildly disheveled, his voice was high pitched like a whining child. Around his bruised neck he word a band of Treeganaut talons. His eyes were frantically darting around as if someone or something were pursuing him. When he finally sat down, an advisor with a long beard, sunken eyes, and a gnarled body approached him. "What did you see, my emperor? Tell me your vision."

Sutin gazed piercingly at his advisor, then at the wall. He exclaimed, "I had a dream that end of the world has come. A ghost kept shouting, 'You are nobody! The day of doom is here. You are nobody!'".

The advisor, shaking his head in mock solemnity, answered, "My emperor, it was just a bad dream. Some phantom of your imagination or a tainted piece of meat. Do not worry yourself."

Sutin, in no mood for condescending explanations, turned on his advisor, demanding, "Would you barter your life on that counsel?"

The advisor appeared stunned, replying more submissively, "I am certain, my Lord."

This affirmation might have helped pacify the emperor if the dungeon guards hadn't brought Atmun, Cadecus, and Deudal into the center of the chamber at that precise moment.

Sutin recognized Atmun instantly as the prophet in his dream and was frightened even more now. The guards, however, weren't aware of the events that had just taken place before their appearance with their three prisoners. After knocking Atmun to the floor, they demanded that he speak his name. "Tell the emperor your name!" one guard sneered gleefully.

"I am nobody," Atmun said.

The guards, who were expecting the entire court to break out into peals of laughter, were horrified to discover that the emperor was enraged. He immediately ordered the dungeon guards arrested. He glared at Atmun.

Suddenly, in an uncontrollable frenzy, the delirious emperor abruptly lunged at Atmun, dashing his head against the ivory floor. This was the moment for all Atmun's friends to rally to his side. They all attempted to separate Sutin from his half-conscious victim, but the remaining palace guards prevailed against them.

Soon, a violent, chaotic scene was unfolding. Minerva, who like Sita was still undetectable, created a hellish vision that terrified the entire assembly.

In this demonic projection, towering flames and fiendish cries swept through the palace overwhelming everyone with feelings of horror and dread. Cadecus, expecting Minerva would act, liberated Atmun from Sutin who was reeling around like a wounded beast. Deudal, at last, found an outlet for his intense rage and threw off the disoriented dungeon guards even though he actually believed that Minerva's terrifying conjuring was real.

The entire castle was soon in a state of turmoil. Soldiers and servants were deserting their stations, shouting hysterically as they endeavored to lower the castle drawbridge. The imaginary inferno and piercing screams pervaded every chamber with horrifying intensity, overcoming Sutin physically and mentally.

Encouraged by her success, Minerva expanded her enchantment beyond the castle walls, throughout the village and into the countryside. The noxious spell's greatly amplified effect engulfed the sentinels and the villagers with the same chaotic cloud inundating the castle. Soon the entire kingdom of Sutin was under siege, controlled by Minerva who seemed almost possessed herself by her own incantation. Her only connection outside her powerful illusion was Sita standing beside her.

As Minerva's elaborate deception grew more vivid, Sutin, fearing for his own safety, approached Atmun in utter despair. His countenance appeared as if he were frightened nearly to death. His advisors fled his side in terror. Sutin again asked Atmun to reveal his identity. "Who are you?" he cried out

The Thought Healer intervened before Atmun could respond. "He is nobody like all the rest of us."

The Thought Healer's remark had a strangely calming effect on the tyrant. He stood suddenly quiet amid the chaotic vision, his fear subsided. He removed the Treeganaut necklace from around his swollen neck. Minerva slowly dissolved her terrifying spell. It was a transformational moment for Sutin.

In his moment of terror and despair, he felt a sense of freedom beyond his kingdom and even his mortal frame. It suddenly occurred to him that immortality was already the condition of all beings. The emperor's induced delusion, in the nightmare and Minerva's horrific drama, pushed him out of his selfishness into a world of peace and silence, previously unknown to him.

Equally astonishing, Atmun had also been deeply affected by his response to Minerva's spell casting. By following the Thought Healer's instructions, Atmun had learned the secret of his identify at last. Even as Sutin had wrestled him to the ground, he chanted 'I am nobody', remaining focused. Then the miraculous happened. As Atmun hit the ground, he surrendered his mind to the river of energy within himself. For one brief moment, he merged with the ocean of Light and Bliss pulsating everywhere within him. When he returned to his body a few moments later, Cadecus was lifting him up and calling his name

It was quite sometime before Minerva's fiendish spectacle dissipated. By then Atmun was better able to feel compassion for Sutin and his state of mind. The emperor's appearance was much more subdued, even repentant.

But Deudal was far less understanding. As soon as he was able, he lunged at Sutin and probably would have killed him if the others hadn't stopped him. "You are a fiend!" the birdman yelled. "Now all my people are dead! Dead! Because of you!"

After Cadecus and the soldiers rescued Sutin from Deudal's razor-sharp grip, Sutin made a stunning revelation. "You're Treeganaut friends aren't dead. They're imprisoned on one of my islands."

"That's a lie! What about the stuffed trophies and jewelry?" Deudal challenged.

"They weren't murdered," Sutin replied meekly. "I scavenged the trophies. Those bird beings were already dead before we kidnapped any of the others. The truth is the talons don't grant immortality. If they did, I would have slept much better at night."

Deudal still agitated, but also hopeful for the first time in years, demanded the emperor reveal the exact location where his people were being held captive. Without a moment's hesitation, Sutin answered, "I will do better than that. I will bring them to you, right here, right now."

The chastened emperor took a hollow reed from his back pocket and began whistling a high pitched sound. It became so intense, it was impossible to endure without covering the ears. At the same time, Minerva and Sita walked out of their invisible space and approached the others. A few minutes later, as Sutin put down his pipe and began describing his newly acquired understanding of life, the sky grew dark as midnight as singing chants filled the air. It was the Treeganauts.

Over a thousand birdlike beings descended on the castle, swooping down to the turrets and gliding to the ground. Soon, they were searching every corridor seeking out the last relative who had been left behind. Somehow they knew that Deudal's courage and perseverance had been at least partly responsible for their liberation. Deudal seemed to recognize every single individual of his race. Before long the entire castle resembled a gigantic aviary.

Once the reunion was complete, there was still the dangerous problem of Sutin and his warriors. It didn't seem prudent to allow Sutin to remain in power, especially since he was the architect of such a monstrous kingdom. Even his promise to reform himself seemed too hasty a conversion for one whose entire life had been one of deceit and conquest.

Deudal didn't believe Sutin's conversion was plausible. The very idea that a wicked tyrant could forever change his actions was not something that Deudal was willing to believe. The emperor's treachery and deceit were notorious in the Graganite kingdom. Deudal was deeply suspicious of Sutin's seemingly genuine change of heart.

As he gazed at the Treeganaut multitude, together at last, Deudal understood Sutin could have easily massacred them at any time, when they were prisoners in his so-called "island" dungeons.

Whether it was protecting his people or seeking revenge, Deudal finally decided to act, ending the threat to his race permanently. As everyone was on the verge of celebrating, and Cadecus and the others, were about to depart from the castle, the giant birdman suddenly rushed over to the emperor and pulled him into the sky.

Gripping him with his talons, Deudal ascended mercilessly. Sutin shrieking in fear, pleading for his life. Deudal, flying high above the clouds, suddenly dropped him. The emperor plummeted to his death. Everyone present was sickened by Deudal's unforeseen wickedness and brutality.

Everyone except the Treeganauts. They were crying out in triumph at the tyrant's death. Their incarceration on the islands with no sky or clouds to glide and swoop across had left them miserable for countless years. Witnessing Sutin's death, they were overwhelmed with joy and gratitude. They all rushed to Deudal and raised him on their shoulders as a conquering hero. As the initial excitement abated, Deudal approached Cadecus and the others saying, "I don't know if you agree with what I've just done, but eliminating Sutin has offered my people freedom and peace. Our world is redeemed, now that the tyrant is dead."

"Yes!" Cadecus suddenly burst out. "You replaced one tyrant with a new one! Your first official act as a leader, Deudal, has been to execute your enemy!"

"But Cadecus," Deudal said, "My people are now safe. From now on we will rule Htrae with compassion."

Cadecus had seen and heard enough. As he and the others turned to leave, he had one last poignant remark. "Just remember, Deudal. You, yourself have committed murder, so now you cannot live as a Treeganaut, forever. You also believe your own race to be the most important. How can you think you have the necessary qualities of humility and compassion to be a truly just ruler?"

Deudal felt hurt by Cadecus's caustic remarks, but he also realized that no amount of persuasion would alter the Thought Healer's opinion. Although he didn't regret his decision to kill Sutin, he did feel dejected realizing he would never see Cadecus again. Nevertheless, his Treeganaut race clearly did understand his motives and their love and support would help him to overcome his sadness.

With nothing more to say, Cadecus, Minerva, Atmun, and Sita headed to the drawbridge in silence. The climax to their mission was far from satisfactory. One evil tyrant had been replaced by a possible despot.

Hopefully Deudal would be a wiser and more compassionate leader than Sutin; but Deudal had the character traits of anger and revenge. These failings could blossom into hatred over time. The future of the Graganite Kingdom was in doubt yet again. Maybe things would get better, but the kingdom itself would certainly not become a utopian society.

The final scene of the Thought Healer's drama was yet to unfold. As they were all stepping across the gap between the drawbridge and the far side of the moat, Sita fell through the open space and bumped her head, immediately losing external consciousness.

When Sita woke up, she found herself sitting in a beautiful rock cavern high in the recesses of the Dhala Mountains. All around her was a tangible stillness, interrupted only by a small crackling fire beside her. She felt an immediate tranquility, deeply inspired by her surroundings. As she acclimated herself to the gentle sounds from the fire, she felt a sense of freedom. In her silent stillness, Sita could even hear her own breath and feel the rhythm of her joyous heart. She held the vision diligently until the Great Being appeared to her.

"You have done well," the Thought Healer whispered. "You have found that the mind creates the worlds. At last, you've arrived here, beyond the worlds of selfishness."

"Where is 'here'?" Sita asked respectfully.

"This realm is the clarity of your own mind," Cadecus answered. "All the stories and characters we create are just illusions and dreams, which exist in space and time as nobody and everybody."

"How can you say we create our experiences?" Sita asked.

"You must know my name, child," Cadecus answered shaping the conversation.

"I am you. You separated yourself from me. All the trials, triumphs, and defeats are really the thoughts and feelings you experienced in order to understand and finally reach this mountain retreat."

"So none of my experiences are real?" Sita asked in confusion

"No, child. Only the Light and Love are real," Cadecus replied. "Everything else exists in the world of change. They are impermanent worlds through which we pass."

"Please, Cadecus," Sita implored. "Explain it an easier way."

"All right," Cadecus asserted. "Most of the individuals of the Htrae world are asleep, but they don't realize it. Some are partially awake, and a few are wide awake. You discovered my image because you were partly awake, so there was real hope for you."

"Are you saying that most people are living in the dark as if they were dreaming?" Sita asked.

"Yes," Cadecus conceded. "Now you have a choice. Do you wish to remain here in happiness and safety, or do you wish to help the dreamers awaken?"

Sita was quiet for a long time pondering the implications of the Thought Healer's question. Finally, she said, "Shouldn't we wish for everyone to wake up, even if it's painful for us at times?"

"Yes," Cadecus agreed warmly. "We must also remember no one can harm our true selves."

As the setting sun sank lower in the sky outside the mouth of the cave, twilight created shadows on the dimming wall. "I am ready to travel again," Sita said softly. "I wish to help others who need to find their way."

"So be it," replied Cadecus.

"When will we leave?" Sita asked with anticipation.

"Is *now* soon enough?" the Thought Healer replied.

List of Topics by Chapter

It's not possible to have a true index since different book formats have different page numbers.

I have substituted this list of the topic headings in each chapter.

1. Brief Autobiography

2. Making Decisions about Medications

Acceptance and Adjustment

Side Effects - Physical

Side Effects - Relationships

Alcohol

Education

Time of Life Impacts

Quality of Life

Why Medications?

The Truth is Simple and Clear to Me Now...

A Few More Words on Challenges

3. 10 Observations about Bipolar Disorder

1. Bipolar Disorder Defined

2. Personal Attitude Changes

3. Onset Effects for Young Adults

4. Importance of Medications

5. Medications : Weight Gain

6. Medications : Quality of Life

7. Medications : Some Issues

4. Coping Strategies: Developing Lines of Defense

5. 10 Valuable Coping Strategies

6. Psychology: Limitations and Benefits

Mental Illness as a Psychological Crisis – The "Model" of Treatment

Counseling

General Knowledge

Personal Understanding

Social Impacts

Precipitating Factors / Triggering Events

Projection

7. Creativity: A Malady and a Remedy

Contains multiple references to Chapter 5

8. 10 Reasons Creativity is so Important to Develop

Contains multiple references to Chapter 5

1. Clarifies Thoughts
2. Increases Self-Knowledge
3. Enhances Concentration
4. Lowers Stress And Enhances Self-Confidence
5. Personal Discovery
6. Resolves The Effects Of Difficult Experiences
7. Openness To New Experiences And Possibilities
8. Generating Original Ideas
9. Exploring Other World Views
10. Expanded Awareness

About the Author

John has faced the challenges of bipolar and anxiety disorder his entire adult life. Over the years he has gradually learned ways to improve his overall health through medication, physical exercise, meditation and creative writing - all vital to his long term recovery. His transformation through spiritual discovery has given his life a greater sense of purpose. John had a 35 year career as a teacher and counselor. Now retired, he spends his days writing poems and stories. Born in upstate New York, he has an M.A. in English from Western Illinois University. He and his wife, Donna, have been married for over forty years.

Website: Contact John
https://www.portalstoinnerdimensions.com/

Facebook: "Friend" John
https://www.facebook.com/writerjohnfzurn/

Books By John Frederick Zurn

<u>Mental Illness Experiences</u>
> The End Justifies the Pain
> The Promise of Long Term Recovery
> The Bipolar Challenge
> Memoirs of a Bipolar Soul
> Metamorphosis:
> from Mental Illness to Spiritual Awakening

<u>Spiritual Experiences</u>
> This Moment Called God
> Passing Through the Dream
> One Hundred Devotional Poems
> Poems of Hope and Inspiration
> 100 Simple Prayers

Fiction: Sojourners Through Time
> *Non-Fiction:* The Comedy in Everyday Life

Don't miss out!

Visit the website below and you can sign up to receive emails whenever John Frederick Zurn publishes a new book. There's no charge and no obligation.

https://books2read.com/r/B-A-IHPT-HPFIC

Did you love *The Promise of Long Term Recovery*? Then you should read *The End Justifies the Pain : Writings About Mental Health*[1] by John Frederick Zurn!

[2]

John chronicles some of his bipolar episode experiences, both in-patient and outpatient;, and how he has achieved long term recovery. He details the process of identifying the appropriate medication and the importance of consistent usage. He identifies a variety of coping skills - how to develop and use them. John then delves into how creative expression can channel thoughts and emotions in useful and constructive ways, psychological and spiritual. As examples of John's creative process, he includes 2 of his short stories and 17 poems.

Read more at https://www.portalstoinnerdimensions.com/.

1. https://books2read.com/u/md68RW

2. https://books2read.com/u/md68RW